CONTENTS

THE BERKELEY SERIES IN AMERICAN HISTORY

The Paxton Riots and the Frontier Theory

Edited by

WILBUR R. JACOBS
UNIVERSITY OF CALIFORNIA, SANTA BARBARA

RAND McNALLY & COMPANY·CHICAGO

The Berkeley Series in American History
Charles Sellers, editor

Rand McNally

INTRODUCTION

DURING THE EIGHTEENTH CENTURY A POWERFUL WAVE OF SETTLEMENT swept through the British North American colonies. Thousands of non-English settlers flowed into the middle colonies of Pennsylvania, New York, and New Jersey. In the Quaker colony itself whole towns and communities underwent a peaceful invasion by German settlers. Following on the heels of the Germans came the Scotch-Irish from Ulster, who in the 1750's carved out homesteads for themselves amid the forests along Pennsylvania's wide frontier. These energetic, restless immigrants, led by their Presbyterian ministers, pushed back the wilderness with axes and plows in an eager search for farmlands—a search which necessarily brought them into armed conflict with the Indians.

The confrontation between Indian and settler was not viewed in its own time as the black-and-white moral issue which it often seems to us today. The frontier settlers were repeatedly victims of Indian savagery (by 1763, the time of Pontiac's uprising, some two thousand of the Scotch-Irish had been killed or taken prisoner), but at the same time the settlers were themselves guilty of violence, for they murdered not simply in self-defense but frequently out of a greed for land, the satisfaction of which depended on the subjection of the Indians. Back in the relative safety of the eastern part of Pennsylvania lived the more "civilized" earlier settlers, the Quakers and other pacific groups, who were horrified at the brutal behavior of the frontier colonists and who opposed their demands for aggressive action against the Indians and a return to scalp payments. But these easterners were not, like the pioneers of Paxton, faced with the daily peril of frontier life.

Obviously the moral issues in such a situation are not simple; yet they merit the attention we pay them, for the relationship between morality and necessity is by no means merely a concern of the past. Obviously, too, this clash between the frontiersmen and the eastern settlers is likely to engage our sympathy on one side or the other, encouraging us to moral assessments of the actions and viewpoints of the various participants. But there are other ways of approaching this historical incident. It is possible to step back from the event, to view it as part of a process which transformed colonial America into the America of today. It is possible to look beyond the specific events to the trends that lie behind them. The Paxton riots and the events surrounding them provide a particularly suitable subject for the study of what the historian Frederick Jackson Turner in his frontier theory called the "processes" of history.

Pennsylvania in the early 1760's was prey to "sectional antagonisms" (another Turnerian concept). Presbyterian Scotch-Irish felt an ingrained antagonism toward the Anglican church and the English politics of the settlers to the east, and they did not have any special affection for the pacifist German sects who, along with the Quaker party, dominated politics in Philadelphia. On top of this, the Scotch-Irish, who had suffered so terribly from barbaric Indian assaults during the French and Indian War, complained that the Quaker-dominated assembly in Philadelphia was not providing them with the necessary protection against their hated enemy. The Paxton Boys (Paxton was a frontier hamlet on the east bank of the Susquehanna River) took matters into their own hands by massacring a group of friendly Indians whom they suspected of treachery and by marching with their supporters to Philadelphia to kill the Indians who had found protection there.

But the differences between the colonials of the interior and those of the eastern seaboard went beyond questions of security. What the settlers at the frontier wanted was democratic representation in their elected assembly, which would assure them of a more effective voice in their government and, they hoped, a better lot in life. To this end they demanded the abolition of the property qualifications for voting. The Paxton rioters insisted on a revision of the apportionment system which permitted eastern counties and the city of Philadelphia to elect twenty-six delegates while the frontier counties had but ten. Other sources of friction were the financial indebtedness of the impoverished frontiersmen to the eastern monied classes and the problems raised by the clash of religions. In Pennsylvania it was Quakerism versus Presbyterianism. Thus behind the immediate question of security from Indian attack lay all the ramifications of a deep-rooted sectional rivalry—a rivalry which does much to explain why it was that the Paxton riots in Pennsylvania almost erupted into civil war.

The idea of sectional rivalry is not the only concept of Turner's which we can see at work in the Paxton riots. Turner believed that American democracy owed more to the presence of free land on the frontier, drawing settlers away from the East and from the more established patterns of life, than it did to the inherited European culture. The frontiersmen of Paxton, faced with life in the wilderness and pulled toward the undeveloped land to the West, did not react as did their fellow Pennsylvanians to the East. Their needs and demands were different, and eventually, perhaps inevitably, the various matters under dispute were settled in favor of the pioneers. Turner, in his famous essay of 1893 on "The Significance of the Frontier in American History," described how the frontier was the prime force in moulding a new American type; the men of Paxton help us to understand more exactly how that change came about.

I

THE BACKGROUND
OF THE RIOTS

THE WINTER OF 1763 WAS A HARD ONE FOR THE MEN OF PAXTON WHO had to fight off repeated Indian raids and whose wives and children were among the victims of the marauding savages. It is hardly surprising that hatred of the Indian was at fever pitch.

Some fifty miles from Paxton was the "manor" of Conestoga, a village of huts belonging to the Conestoga Indians, who lived by begging and by selling baskets and brooms. Most settlers regarded the Conestogas as harmless, for they had lived in harmony with the Quaker colony for almost a century. But at Paxton it was rumored that these Indians were spies and were giving shelter to war parties, and in any case the Paxton Boys were in no mood to discriminate between friendly and hostile Indians.

On the morning of December 14, 1763, Matthew Smith, the leader of the Paxton Boys, led his armed, mounted men to Conestoga where they burst into the native cabins and butchered three men, two women, and a child. Fourteen Indians who escaped the wrath of the frontiersmen were taken into protective custody by the Pennsylvania government and housed at the nearby Lancaster town jail.

But the rage of the Paxton Boys was not satisfied by their sixfold murder. Furious that some of their intended victims had escaped, they galloped into Lancaster on December 27, smashed open the door of the jail, and killed the fourteen remaining Indians, leaving the bodies of men, women, and children scattered about the jailhouse yard. When news of the massacres reached Philadelphia not only the Scotch-Irish rioters but the whole Presbyterian sect was held responsible for what had happened.

Meanwhile, about 125 additional Indians, many of whom had been converted to Christianity by the Moravians, were being sheltered in Philadelphia. Here they were supplied with food by the Moravian brethren while the assembly debated the desirability of sheltering Indians in the city.

On the frontier it seemed almost intolerable that the Philadelphia assembly should virtually ignore the sufferings of the pioneers at Paxton and at the same time pay for the keep of Indian fugitives. The Paxton Boys resolved, therefore, to march on Philadelphia in order to do away with these protected Indians. But by the time they had advanced on the provincial capital, the city had been transformed into an armed camp under the leadership of Benjamin Franklin. Church bells rang and drums rolled, streets were barricaded and cannons mounted. Even some of the Quakers shouldered arms. The rioters halted their march at Germantown, some six miles from the city. To this spot came Benjamin Franklin and other Philadelphians who had been asked by the governor and council to try to persuade the insurgents to turn back. In this they were successful. Two representatives of the Paxton Boys stayed behind to draw up a statement of grievances for the consideration of the governor and assembly.

Once the crisis was past (to the great relief of the townspeople), the assembly did little more than debate the declaration of grievances. Equal representation in the assembly, the principal demand of the Paxton Boys, had to wait for the assembly act of March 23, 1776, several months before the Declaration of Independence.

The following documents set out the assembly's frontier defense policy and the reactions to the policy before the outbreak of the riots.

A.

FRONTIER DEFENSE POLICY OF THE PENNSYLVANIA ASSEMBLY, 1763

❡The assembly defended itself in this message against charges of neglecting frontier defenses against Indian attack, charges which had been brought against it by Sir Jeffery Amherst, commander-in-chief of military forces in the colonies, and Sir William Johnson, northern Indian superintendent. (*"Minutes of the Provincial Council of Pennsylvania from the Organization to the Termination of the Proprietary Government," Pennsylvania Colonial Records,* 16 vols. [Harrisburg, 1852], IX, 64-66.)

What criticisms were made of the assembly defense policy?
How did the assembly answer the criticisms?]

A Message to the Governor from the Assembly.

MAY IT please your Honour:
We return you our thanks for laying before us the Letter you have received from Sir Jeffery Amherst, of the Sixteenth of this Inst^(t.,) with the Intelligence inclosed therein, from S^(r.) William Johnson, respecting the bad intentions of the Savages against our Frontiers. For this Intelligence We are likewise obliged to His Excellency, but at the same time we are greatly at a loss how to understand the

meaning or design of that part of his Letter wherein he expresses his "Surprize at the Infatuation of the People of this Province, who (he alledges) tamely look on while their Brethren are butchered by the Savages, when, without doubt, it is in their power, by exerting a proper spirit, not only to protect the Settlements, but to punish any Indians that are hardy enough to disturb them." Can it be possible that the General is, at this day, unacquainted with the vigorous Measures which this Government has pursued, much beyond any of the rest of the Colonies, for the Protection and Defence of their long extended Frontier?

Your Honour well knows, that on the Eleventh of June last, you convened the Provincial Commissioners, who chearfully agreed to raise an hundred Men for the Reinforcement of Fort Augusta, a Garrison on Susquehanna, then but weakly manned, and a Post of great importance to the Provincial Defence.

On the fourth of July the Assembly met, in pursuance of your Summons, when you laid before them the necessity of an Additional number of Men, to repel the savage attempts of those Barbarians; & that, in pursuance of a Letter from the General, which you also communicated to them, with equal Chearfulness and Expedition, they granted the additional number of Seven hundred Men, and passed a Law for furnishing Carriages for the Transportation of Provisions for the use of the Troops destined for the Western Communication.

These Troops, so granted, were accordingly raised with the utmost Expedition, & they have been, as we are informed, placed at proper Stations on the Frontiers, under your Command, and been active since in the protection thereof, and that with more vigour and Spirit than has been known or experienced the whole late War. Several Parties of Indians have been intercepted and repulsed, and the Inhabitants in a great measure preserved from the intended Massacres, and a large Body of them now engaged in an Expedition against the Great Island, which has heretofore served as a Station from whence the Savages usually issue, for the Annoyance of our Settlements.

As these things are Facts, we cannot help, in our Turn, being much surprized at the Censure contained in His Excellency's Letter, by which it is evidently intimated that the good People of this Province are utterly regardless of the Distresses of their Fellow Subjects, and "tamely look on while they are butchered by the Savages."

A hard Censure this! but for what part of the Government it was intended is not clear from the Letter. If intended for your Honour, we have reason to believe you have done everything, as Commander-in-Chief of the Forces, that could be expected. If for this Part of the Legislature, the large number of Men in the pay of this Government, at a time when the Province is loaded with a debt extremely burthensome, occasioned by their late generous and large Aids to the Crown for the protection of the Colonies during the late War, will evidently shew it is without foundation; And if the poor People on our Frontiers, their present distressed Situation, and the uncommon Military Spirit & Resolution, so manifest among them ever since the late Indian Incursions, ought at least to have excused them from it.

But the Genl. is of Opinion, that it is in our power, by exerting a proper Spirit, not only to protect the Settlements, but to punish any Indians that are hardy enough to disturb them. Would he give himself the Liberty of one Moment's Reflection on our Circumstances, must he not see the Injustice as well as Impracticability of our defending a Frontier near three hundred Miles in length, which covers and protects, in a great measure, those of Maryland and New Jersey, without the least Contribution or aid from either of those Colonies. Is it reasonable that this Province, already heavily loaded with debt, should be at the Sole Expence of defending not only her own Frontiers but so great a part of those of her neighbouring Colonies? And is it not evidently impossible that this Young Colony, against whom the Indian Force has been principally aimed, should alone, without any assistance from the rest of the Provinces, defend a Frontier so extensive, against all the lurking and perfidious Parties of so powerful a Confederacy as is mentioned in the General's Intelligence.

You, Sir, are well acquainted with the Circumstances of the Province, & its present Distress, and therefore we presume you readily see how vain the Expectation must prove, that any one particular Colony can defend itself against the united Power of so many Confederated Nations.

Signed by order of the House,

ISAAC NORRIS, Speaker.

October 22nd, 1763.

B.

REACTIONS TO THE ASSEMBLY'S POLICY

❮1. *Depositions of Frontiersmen.* Frontiersmen and their families obviously felt insecure when Indians capable of giving secret aid to attacking war parties lived in their vicinity. Following are depositions made by Alexander Stephen and Robert Armstrong containing "Sworn" evidence against Conestoga Indians. (John R. Dunbar, ed., *The Paxton Papers* [The Hague, 1957], p. 197.)

Was the material hearsay or direct evidence?

Did such evidence implicate the Conestoga Indians in a conspiracy against the English?]

LANCASTER COUNTY

Personally appeared before me one of his Majesty's Justices of the Peace for s^d. County, Alexander Stephen, & being qualified as the Law directs, saith that an Indian Woman named Canayah Sally told the s^d. Deponent, since the last War, that the Conestogoe Indians killed Jegrea an Indian Man, because he would not go to War with the s^d. Conestogoe Indians against the English; & that James Cottis told s^d. Deponent since the last War, that he was one of the three, that

[6]

killed old James (or William) Hamilton on Sherman's Creek, the Beginning of the last War. And farther this Deponent saith, that after the late War s^d. James Cottis demanded of s^d. Deponent a Canoe, which he had found, or pay in Lieu thereof, which Canoe the s^d. Murderers had left, as Cottis said, at the Time.

Sworn & subscribed before

Tho. Foster   by Alexander Stephen

LANCASTER COUNTY

Personally appeared before me one of his Majesty's Justices of the Peace for s^d. County, Robert Armstrong, & being qualified as the Law directs saith as follows, Viz. an Indian named Seahaes with several others lived near my House in the Year 1762; some of them were so impudent as to say, that they had been at War with the White People & would soon be at War again, particularly one Isaac, who called Seahaes his Uncle. In the Year 1762 as the Indians were coming down to the Treaty, they happened to stay at my House in Hallifax; a Man whose Name as near as I can remember was William Philips & his Wife, being both Prisoners, told me they would be qualified, that the Indians held two Councils, & agreed that they would go to Philadelphia & get what they could, & so return & cut off the back Settlements. On their Return the s^d. Indians stayed four Days about my Place & proved very insolent, took about six acres of Corn, killed several Hoggs, & took the Fruit of about 150 bearing Trees, and farther saith not

Sworn before Thos.^{s} Foster,

and signed by Robert Armstrong

N.B. Seahaes &. Isaac were Conestogoe Indians.—

[2. *Indian Complaints.* Although the frontier settlers complained about Indian attacks, the Indians themselves had grievances, especially the Conestogas, who said they had "always lived in Peace and Quietness." (*Pennsylvania Colonial Records*, IX, 88-89.)

What were the grievances of the Conestogas?

Was the policy of neutrality to which they adhered beneficial to the Conestogas?]

To the Honourable JOHN PENN, Esquire, Lieutenant Governor and Commander-in-Chief of the Province of Pennsylvania, &ca, &ca.

BROTHER:

We (the Conestogoe Indians) take the present opportunity, by Capt$^n.$ Montour, to welcome you into this Country by this String of Wampum, and as we were settled at this place by an Agreement of Peace and Amity established between your Grandfathers & ours, We now promise ourselves your favour and protection, and as we have always lived in Peace and Quietness with our Brethren & Neighbours round us during the last & present Indian Wars, We hope now, as we are deprived from supporting our Families by hunting, as We formerly did, you will consider our distressed Situation, & grant our Women and Children some Cloathing to cover them this Winter. The Government has always been kind enough to allow us some Provisions, and did formerly appoint People to take care of us, but as there is no person to take that upon him, & some of our Neighbours have encroach'd upon the Tract of Land reserved here for our use, We would now beg our Brother the Governor to appoint our Friend Captain Thomas M'Kee, who lives near us and understands our Language, to take care, and see Justice done us.

SOHAYS, X his Mark.
INDIAN, X his Mark.
or CUYANGUERRYCOEA,
his
SAGUYASOTHA, X or JOHN.
Mark.

Conestogoe, Novr. 30th, 1763.

C.

BEGINNINGS OF THE RIOTS

❡1. *The Conestoga Massacre.* Edward Shippen, magistrate of the town of Lancaster, described the massacre of Conestoga Indians by armed, mounted frontiersmen in his letter of December 14, 1763, to Governor John Penn. (*Pennsylvania Colonial Records*, IX, 89-90.)

How did magistrate Shippen obtain detailed information about the massacre?

What happened to the Indians who escaped?]

LANCASTER, 14th December, 1763, Evening.

HONOURED SIR:

One Robert Edgar, a hired Man to Captain Thomas M'Kee, living near the Borough, acquainted me to-day that a Company of People from the Frontiers had killed and scalped most of the Indians at the Conestogoe Town early this Morning; he said he had his information from an Indian boy who made his Escape; Mr. Slough has been to the place and held a Coroner's Inquest on the Corpses, being Six in number; Bill Sawk and some other Indians were gone towards Smith's Iron Works to sell brooms; but where they are now we can't understand; And the Indians, John Smith, & Peggy, his Wife, and their child, and Young Joe Hays, were abroad last night too, and lodged at one Peter Swar's, about two miles from hence; These last came here this afternoon, whom we acquainted with what had happened to their Friends & Relations, and advised them to put themselves under our Protection, which they readily agreed to; And they are now in Our Work House by themselves, where they are well provided for with every necessary. Warrants are issued for the apprehending of the Murderers, said to be upwards of fifty men, well armed & mounted. I beg my kind Complements to Mr. Richard Penn, & I am with all due Regards,

Sir, Your Honour's Obliged
Friend, and most humble Servant,
EDW^{D.} SHIPPEN.

The Honble JOHN PENN, Esq^{r.,} Governor.

[2. *The Lancaster Massacre.*   Among the Indians who escaped the Paxton Boys's rage at Conestoga was a suspected spy and murderer. At Lancaster, in the workhouse, or jail, the survivors were thought to be secure, but, on December 27, the Paxton Boys broke down the doors and slaughtered the remaining Conestogas. Magistrate Edward Shippen described the massacre in a second letter to Governor Penn on December 27, 1763. (*Pennsylvania Colonial Records*, IX, 100.)

Why were the Conestogas not protected by the Lancaster Sheriff and other officers?

Did the Paxton Boys make an attempt to carry off their suspect without molesting the other Conestogas?]

LANCASTER, 27th Decem^r. 1763, P. M.

HONOURED SIR:

I am to acquaint your Honour that between two and three of the clock this afternoon, upwards of a hundred armed men, from the Westward, rode very fast into Town, turned their Horses into Mr. Slough's (an Inn-keeper) Yard, and proceeded with the greatest Precipitation to the Work House, stove open the door and killed all the Indians, and then took to their Horses and rode off, all their business was done, and they were returning to their horses before I could get half way down to the Work house; The Sheriff and Coroner, however, & several others, got down as soon as the Rioters, but could not prevail with them to stop their hands; some people say they heard them declare they would proceed to the Province Island, and destroy the Indians there.

I am with great Respect, Sir,
Your Honour's most Obedient humble Servant,
EDW^D SHIPPEN.

The Honble Jno. Penn, Esqr., Govr.

[3. *The Governor's Proclamation of January 2, 1764.*   After the Conestoga massacre, Governor Penn had issued a proclamation instructing magistrates of the frontier counties to apprehend the rioters. News of the second massacre thoroughly aroused the people of Philadelphia, and the governor, with the support of the assembly, issued a second proclamation offering a reward for the capture or information leading to the capture of any three "Ringleaders" of the rioters. (*Pennsylvania Colonial Records*, IX, 107-8.)

What was the governor's interpretation of "Justice"?

What judicial procedure did the governor propose for punishment of the "Ringleaders"?]

A Proclamation:

WHEREAS, ON the twenty-second day of December last, I issued a Proclamation for the apprehending and bringing to Justice a number of Persons who, in violation of the Public Faith, & in Defiance of all Law, had inhumanly killed Six of the Indians who had lived on Conestogoe Manor for the Course of many Years, peaceably and inoffensively, under the Protection of this Government, on Lands assigned to them for their Habitation. Notwithstanding which, I have received Information that on the Twenty-seventh of the same Month, a large party of armed Men again assembled and met together in a riotous & tumultous manner, in the County of Lancaster & proceeded to the Town of Lancaster, where they violently broke open the Work House, and butchered and put to death fourteen of the said Conestogoe Indians, Men, Women, and Children, who had been taken under the immediate Care and Protection of the Magistrates of the said County, and lodged for their better Security in the said Workhouse, till they should be more effectually provided for by Order of the Government: *And Whereas*, common Justice loudly demands, and the Laws of the Land, (upon the preservation of which not only the Liberty and Security of every Individual, but the being of the Government itself depend), require that the above Offenders should be brought to condign Punishment; I have, therefore, by and with the advice of the Council, published this Proclamation, & do hereby strictly charge & command all Judges, Justices, Sheriffs, Constables, Officers Civil and Military, and all other his Majesty's faithful and liege Subjects within this Province, to make diligent Search and enquiry after the Authors and Perpetrators of the said last mentioned Offence, their Abettors and Accomplices; and that they use all possible means to apprehend and secure them in some of the public Gaols of this Province, to be dealt with according to Law. And I do hereby further promise and engage, that any Person or Persons who shall apprehend & secure, or cause to be apprehended and secured, any three of the Ringleaders of the said party, and prosecute them to conviction, shall have and receive for each the publick reward of Two Hundred Pounds; and any Accomplice, not concerned in the immediate shedding the Blood of the said Indians, who shall make discovery of any or either of the said Ringleaders & apprehend and prosecute them to conviction, shall, over and above the said Reward, have all the weight and influence of the Government for obtaining his Majesty's Pardon for his Offence.

Given under my hand and the Great Seal of the said Province, at Philadelphia, the second day of January, in the fourth Year of His Majesty's Reign, & in the Year of our Lord, one thousand seven hundred & Sixty-four.

JOHN PENN.

By His Honour's Command.
JOSEPH SHIPPEN, Jun^{r.,} Secretary.
GOD SAVE THE KING.

[4. *The Assembly's Message to the Governor, January 3, 1764.* One day after the governor's proclamation of January 2 offering a reward for the capture of the Paxton leaders, the assembly voted funds for the purpose of frustrating the "further wicked Designs" of the rioters. (*Pennsylvania Colonial Records*, IX, 109-10.)
Why was the assembly so eager to provide funds for the governor's use?]

MAY IT please your Honour:

The House have given their "most serious and immediate Attention to the important Affairs" laid before them in Your Honour's Message of this afternoon, and considering that the military Force of this Province is at present engaged in the defence of our long extended Frontier, by your Honour's orders, have unanimously entered into a vote of Credit that they will make Provision for defraying the Expence of such additional Force as the Governor & present Provincial Commissioners shall find necessary to Frustrate the further wicked Designs of those lawless Rioters who have perpetrated the most inhuman murders on the poor defenceless Indians, ancient Friends of this Province, and living under the Protection of its Government; And they, with pleasure, acquaint your Honour that they are just now informed a considerable sum has lately been paid into the hands of the Treasurer, which may be immediately applied to the purpose of "repelling those bold invaders of Law and Justice, & supporting the Honour and Dignity of the Government," and which will probably be sufficient, 'till such a Bill as your Honour recommends, can be prepared and considered.

Signed by Order of the House,

January 3rd, 1764. ISAAC NORRIS, *Speaker.*

D.

THE RIOTERS MARCH ON PHILADELPHIA

❡ 1. *The City Is Warned.* Although the entire colony of Pennsylvania was seething with rumors, charges, and countercharges concerning the massacres, the chief center of discontent was still the frontier, where armed preparations were being made to march on the city to kill Indians under government protection.

The assembly considered several alternative plans to save the Indians from another massacre. When the governor of New York refused to permit the refugees to enter his province, where they might have lived under the care of Indian superintendent Sir William Johnson, it was decided that they should be lodged in military barracks in Philadelphia under the protection of a regiment of British soldiers.

On January 28, 1764, Benjamin Kendall, a Philadelphia merchant, met with the governor and his council to answer questions about the activities of frontiersmen. Kendall had just returned from Lancaster and carried alarming news about the plans of the Paxton Boys. (*Pennsylvania Colonial Records,* IX, 126-27.)

What did Kendall say about conflicts between Quakers and Presbyterians?

What frontier military plans did Kendall report?

What was the source of Kendall's information? Did it contain possible exaggerations?]

City of Philadelphia:

BENJAMIN KENDALL, of the City of Philadelphia, Merchant, being one of the People called Quakers, on his Solemn Affirmation declareth and saith, That on Thursday, the 26th day of this Instant, January, he, this deponent, being on his return from the Burrough of Lancaster to the City of Philadelphia, about two Miles on this side the sign of the Hat, (a Tavern kept by one Samuel Smith), he met with Robert Fulton, an Inhabitant of the said Burrough of Lancaster, who, this affirmant understood, had been, the day before, in the Township of Pequea, or its Neighborhood; That this affirmant, being acquainted with the said Robert Fulton, stopped, and entered into some Conversation with him, in the course of which the said Fulton acquainted this Affirmant that he understood Captn. Coultas had been appointed to raise and command Five hundred Men, to guard & protect the Indians in the City of Philadelphia, and that he was very sorry for it, and that in ten days fifteen hundred Men would come down in order to kill the said Indians, and that if Fifteen hundred were not enough, Five thousand were ready to join them, and desired this affirmant to tell the said Captain Coultas, from the said Robert, to make his Peace with Heaven, for that he (the said Coultas) would not live above two Weeks longer. This affirmant answered, that he was very sorry to hear him, the said Fulton, talk in that manner, and as he understood that he, the said Fulton, had a good deal of influence with those People, who intended to come down on the above Purpose, he, this affirmant, requested the said Fulton to exert it in persuading them to desist from their Design. The said Fulton then said, If Gabriel was to come down from Heaven and tell *us or them* (but which of the words this affirmant cannot be sensible of) *we or they* were wrong, they would not desist for it, for that they were of the same Spirit with the blood-ran, blood-thirsty Presbyterians, who cut off King Charles his Head. This Affirmant then said to the said Fulton, "I hear you intend to kill the Quakers." Fulton answered, "No, God forbid, but they or any others who should oppose them they would kill." That he (the said Fulton) had heard the Indians were put in small numbers into different Families in the City of Philadelphia, for Protection, but that such Families must tell where they (the Indians) were, and deliver them up, or their Houses would be fired over their heads. The said Fulton further informed this Affirmant, that some time ago, when he heard that the said Indians were sent out of this Province, he, the said Fulton, sent a Letter to a number of People, who were then preparing to come down and cut the Indians off, to acquaint them of it, and stop them from coming. This Affirmant further saith, that a certain William Way was in Company with the said Fulton during this whole Conversation, &, from what little he said, seemed to join in Sentiment with the said Fulton, & among other things asserted, that he was lately in a Store in that Neighbourhood, where there was a Magazine of three half barrels of Gun Powder, and one hundred small Arms, ready for the above Expedition, & that he verily believed a number of Men would come down to Philadelphia to kill the Indians, and further this Affirmant saith not.

BENJ^A· KENDALL.

Taken and Affirmed in the presence of the Governor and Council, at Philadᵃ·· January 28, 1764.
Before

JOHN PENN.

[2. *The Arrival of the Paxton Boys.* On February 5, 1764, some two hundred mounted frontiersmen, armed with rifles, tomahawks, and pistols, approached Germantown on the outskirts of the city of Philadelphia. Here their leaders conferred with a government delegation led by Benjamin Franklin. The promise that their grievances would be put before the provincial parliament finally persuaded them to turn back. A brief account of the incident is given in the following newspaper excerpt. (*The Pennsylvania Gazette,* February 9, 1764.)

How did Philadelphia prepare for an attack by the "Insurgents"?]

PHILADELPHIA, *February 9.*

ON SATURDAY last the City was alarmed with the News of great Numbers of armed Men, from the Frontiers, being on the several Roads, and moving towards Philadelphia. As their Designs were unknown, and there were various Reports concerning them, it was thought prudent to put the City in some posture of Defence against any Outrages that might possibly be intended. The Inhabitants being accordingly called upon by the Governor, great Numbers of them entered into an Association, and took Arms for the Support of Government, and Maintenance of good Order.

Six Companies of Foot, one of Artillery, and 2 Troops of Horse, were formed, and paraded; to which, it is said, some Thousands, who did not appear, were prepared to join themselves, in case any Attempt should be made against the Town. The Barracks also, where the Indians are lodged, under Protection of the regular Troops, were put into a good Posture of Defence; several Works being thrown up about them, and eight Pieces of Cannon planted there.

The Insurgents, it seems, intended to rendezvous at Germantown; but the Precautions taken at the several Ferries over Schuylkill impeded their Junction; and those who assembled there, being made acquainted with the Force raised to oppose them, listened to the reasonable Discourses and Advice of some prudent Persons, who voluntarily went out to meet and admonish them; and of some Gentlemen sent by the Governor, to know the Reasons of their Insurrection; and promised to return peaceably to their Habitations, leaving only two of their Number to present a Petition to the Governor and Assembly; on which the Companies raised in Town were thanked by the Governor on Tuesday Evening, and dismissed, and the City restored to its former Quiet.

But on Wednesday Morning there was a fresh Alarm, occasioned by a false Report, that Four Hundred of the same People were on their March to Attack the Town: Immediately, on Beat of Drum, a much greater Number of the Inhabitants, with the utmost Alacrity, put themselves under Arms; but as the Truth was soon known, they were again thanked by the Governor, and dismissed; the Country People being really dispersed, and gone home according to their Promise.

II

THE NATURE OF THE RIOTS

ALTHOUGH THE PAXTON RIOTS OF THE WINTER OF 1763 WERE SPARKED by conflict with the Indians, a larger conflict was developing between the frontier counties and the provincial government—a conflict, moreover, in which religious overtones soon appeared.

The documents in this chapter discuss the disputed issues from the point of view of the frontiersmen and from that of the Quakers.

A.

GRIEVANCES OF THE RIOTERS

❡ 1. *The Declaration.* The *Declaration,* composed by the representatives of the Paxton Boys who had been elected at Germantown, told the story of the massacres from the viewpoint of the frontier, charging that the government "openly caressed" hostile Indians and declined to provide for adequate defense. (*Pennsylvania Colonial Records,* IX, 142-45.)

How did the frontiersmen justify the massacre of the Indians? What criticisms were made of government policy?]

The Declaration of the injured Frontier Inhabitants, together with a brief sketch of Grievances the good Inhabitants of the Province labour under.

INASMUCH AS the killing those Indians at Conestogoe Manor and Lancaster has been, and may be, the subject of much Conversation, and by invidious Representations of it, which some, we doubt not, will industriously spread, many unacquainted with the true state of Affairs may be led to pass a Severe Censure on the Authors of those Facts, and any others of the like nature, which may hereafter happen, than we are persuaded they would if matters were duly understood and deliberated. We think it, therefore, proper thus openly to declare ourselves, and render some brief hints of the reasons of our Conduct, which we must, and frankly do, confess, nothing but necessity itself could induce us to, or justify us in, as it bears an appearance of flying in the face of Authority, and is attended with much labour, fatigue, and expence.

Ourselves, then, to a Man, we profess to be loyal Subjects to the best of Kings, our rightful Sovereign George the third, firmly attached to his Royal Person, Interest, and Government, & of consequence, equally opposite to the Enemies of His Throne & Dignity, whether openly avowed, or more dangerously concealed under a mask of falsly pretended Friendship, and chearfully willing to offer our Substance & Lives in his Cause.

These Indians, known to be firmly connected in Friendship with our openly avowed embittered Enemies, and some of whom have, by several Oaths, been proved to be murderers, and who, by their better acquaintance with the Situation and State of our Frontier, were more capable of doing us mischief, we saw, with indignation, cherished and caressed as dearest Friends; But this, alas! is but a part, a small part, of that excessive regard manifested to Indians, beyond His Majesty's loyal Subjects, whereof we complain, and which, together with various other Grievances, have not only enflamed with resentment the Breasts of a number, and urged them to the disagreeable Evidence of it they have been constrained to give, but have heavily displeased by far the greatest part of the good Inhabitants of this Province.

Should we here reflect to former Treaties, the exorbitant presents and great Servility therein paid to Indians, have long been oppressive Grievances we have groaned under; and when at the last Indian Treaty held at Lancaster, not only was the Blood of our many murdered Brethren tamely covered, but our poor unhappy captivated Friends abandoned to slavery among the Savages, by concluding a Friendship with the Indians, and allowing them a plenteous trade of all kinds of Commodities, without those being restored, or any properly spirited Requisition made of them; How general Dissatisfaction those Measures gave, the Murmurs of all good People (loud as they dare to utter them) to this day declare, and had here infatuated Steps of Conduct, and a manifest Partiality in favour of Indians, made a final pause, happy had it been; We perhaps had grieved in silence for our abandoned, enslaved Brethren among the Heathen; but matters of a later Date are still more flagrant Reasons of Complaint. When last Summer His Majesty's Forces, under the Command of Colonel Bouquet, marched through this Province, and a demand was made by His Excellency General Amherst, of Assistance to escort Provisions, &ca., to relieve that important Post, Fort Pitt, yet not one man was granted, although never any thing appeared more reasonable or necessary, as the interest of the Province lay so much at stake, and the standing of the Frontier Settlements, in any manner, evidently depended, under God, on the almost despaired of success of His Majesty's little Army, whose Valour the whole Frontiers with gratitude acknowledge, and as the happy means of having saved from ruin great part of the Province; But when a number of Indians, falsely pretended Friends, and having among them some proved on Oath to have been guilty of Murder since this War begun, when they, together with others, known to be His Majesty's Enemies, and who had been in the Battle against Col. Bouquet, reduced to Distress by the Destruction of their Corn at the Great Island, and up the East branch of Susquehanna, pretend themselves Friends, and desire a Subsistance, they are openly caressed, & the Publick, that could not be indulged the liberty of contributing to His Majesty's assistance, obliged, as Tributaries to Savages, to support these Villians, these Enemies to our King & our Country; nor only so, but the hands that were closely shut, nor would grant His Majesty's General a single Farthing against a Savage Foe, have been liberally opened, and the Publick money basely prostituted to hire, at an exorbitant Rate, a mercenary Guard to protect His Majesty's worst of Enemies, those falsly pretended Indian friends, while, at the same time, Hundreds of poor distressed Families of His Majesty's Subjects, obliged to abandon their Possessions & fly for their lives at least, are left, except a small Relief at first, in the most distressing Circumstances, to starve neglected, save what the friendly hand of private Donations has contributed to their support, wherein they who are most profuse towards Savages, have carefully avoided having any part. When last Summer the Troops raised for Defence of the Province were limited to certain Bounds, nor suffered to attempt annoying our Enemies in their Habitations, and a number of brave Volunteers, equipped at their own Expence in September, up the Susquehanna, met and defeated their Enemy, with the loss of some of their number, and having others dangerously wounded, not the least thanks or acknowledgment was made them from the Legislature for the confessed Service they had done, nor only the least notice or Care taken of their wounded; Whereas, when a Seneca, who, by the Informany of many, as well as by his own Confession, had been, through the last War, our inveterate Enemy, had got a cut in his Head, last Summer, in a quarrel he had with his own Cousin, & it was reported in Philadelphia that his Wound was dangerous, a Doctor was immediately employed and sent to Fort Augusta to take care of him, and cure him if possible. To these may be added, that though it was impossible to obtain, through the Summer, or even yet, any Premium for Indian Scalps, or encouragement to excite Volunteers to go forth against them; Yet, when a few of them known to be the fast friends of our Enemies, and some of them murderers themselves, when these have been struck by a distressed, bereft, injured Frontier, a liberal reward is offered for apprehending the Perpetrators of that horrible Crime of Killing his Majesty's Cloaked Enemies, and their Conduct painted in the most atrocious Colours, while the horrid Ravages, cruel murders, and most shocking Barbarities, committed by Indians on His Majesty's Subjects, are covered over, and excused, under the charitable Term of this being their method of making War. But to recount the many repeated Grievances, whereof we might justly complain, and instances of a most violent attachment to Indians, were tedious beyond the patience of a Job to endure, nor can better be

[17]

expected, nor need we be surprized at Indians insolence & Villainy, when it is considered, and which can be proved from the Publick Records of a certain County, that sometime before Conrad Weiser died, some Indians belonging to the Great Island or Wighalousing, assured him that Israel Pemberton (an ancient leader of that Faction, which for so long a time have found means to enslave the Province to Indians), together with others of the Friends, had given them a Rod to scourge the White People that were settled on the purchased Lands, for that Onas had cheated them out of a great deal of Land, or had not given near sufficient Price for what he had bought; and that the Traders ought also to be scourged, for that they defrauded the Indians, by selling Goods to them at too dear a rate; and that this Relation is matter of Fact, can easily be proved in the County of Berks. Such is our unhappy Situation, under the Villainy, Infatuation and Influence of a certain Faction, that have got the Political Reins in their hands, and tamely tyrannize over the other good Subjects of the Province. And can it be thought strange, that a Scene of such treatment as this, & the now adding, in this critical Juncture, to all our former Distresses, that disagreeable Burthen of supporting, in the very heart of the Province, at so great an Expence, between one and two hundred Indians, to the great Disquietude of the Majority of the good Inhabitants of this Province, should awaken the resentment of a people grossly abused, unrighteously burthened, and made Dupes and Slaves to Indians? And must not all well disposed people entertain a charitable Sentiment of those who, at their own great Expence and Trouble, have attempted or shall attempt, rescuing a labouring Land from a Weight so oppressive, unreasonable and unjust? It is this we design, it is this we are resolved to prosecute, though it is with great Reluctance we are obliged to adopt a Measure not so agreeable as could be desired, and to which Extremity alone compels.

GOD SAVE THE KING.

[2. *The Remonstrance.* This document, listing nine complaints, was also written by representatives of the Paxton Boys on behalf of the frontier counties. What the settlers on the frontier wanted above all was a just apportionment of places in the provincial legislature. Other areas of dispute were Indian policy and scalp payments. A demand for more effective aid from the garrison of the frontier post, Fort Augusta, closed the list. (*Pennsylvania Colonial Records,* IX, 138-42.)

Why did the frontier counties wish to change the apportionment in the assembly?

Were the demands for changes in Indian policy made by the frontiersmen justified in the light of life on the frontier? How was the assembly likely to view these demands?]

To the Honourable JOHN PENN, Esquire, Governor of the Province of Pennsylvania & of the Counties of New Castle, Kent, and Sussex, on Delaware, and to the Representatives of the Freemen of the said Province, in General Assembly met:

We, Matthew Smith and James Gibson, in behalf of ourselves and His Majesty's faithful and loyal Subjects, the Inhabitants of the Frontier Counties of Lancaster, York, Cumberland, Berks, and Northampton, humbly beg leave to remonstrate & lay before you the following Grievances, which we submit to your Wisdom for Redress.

First. We apprehend that as Freemen and English Subjects, we have an indisputable Title to the same Privileges & immunities with His Majesty's other Subjects who reside in the interior Counties of Philadelphia, Chester, and Bucks, and therefore ought not to be excluded from an equal share with them in the very important Privilege of Legislation; nevertheless, contrary to the Proprietors Charter and the acknowledged principles of common Justice & Equity, our five Counties are restrained from electing more than ten Representatives, viz^r.: four for Lancaster, two for York, two for Cumberland, one for Berks, and one for Northampton, while the three Counties and City of Philadelphia, Chester, and Bucks, elect Twenty-Six. This we humbly conceive is oppressive, unequal, and unjust, the cause of many of our Grievances, and an infringement of our Natural privileges of Freedom & Equality; wherefore, we humbly pray that we may be no longer deprived of an equal number with the three aforesaid Counties, to represent us in Assembly.

Secondly. We understand that a Bill is now before the House of Assembly, wherein it is provided that such Persons as shall be charged with killing any Indians in Lancaster County, shall not be tried in the County where the Fact was committed, but in the Counties of Philadelphia, Chester or Bucks. This is manifestly to deprive British Subjects of their known Privileges, to cast an eternal Reproach upon whole Counties, as if they were unfit to serve their Country in the quality of Jurymen, and to contradict the well known Laws of the British Nation in a point whereon Life, Liberty and security essentially depend, namely, that of being tried by their equals in the neighborhood where their own, their Accusers, and the Witnesses' Character and Credit, with the Circumstances of the Fact, are best known, & instead thereof putting their Lives in the hands of Strangers, who may as justly be suspected of partiallity to as the Frontier Counties can be of prejudices against Indians; and this, too, in favour of Indians only, against His Majesty's faithful & loyal Subjects. Besides, it is well known that the design of it is to comprehend a Fact committed before such a Law was thought of. And if such practices were tolerated, no man could be secure in his most valuable Interest. We are also informed, to our great Surprize, that this Bill has actually received the assent of a Majority of the House, which we are persuaded could not have been the case, had our Frontier Counties been equally represented in Assembly. However, we hope that the Legislature of this Province will never enact a Law of so dangerous a tendency, or take away from his Majesty's good Subjects a privilege so long esteemed sacred by Englishmen.

Thirdly. During the late and present Indian War, the Frontiers of this Province have been repeatedly attacked and ravaged by Skulking parties of the Indians, who have with the most Savage Cruelty murdered

Men, Women and Children, without distinction, and have reduced near a thousand Families to the most extream distress. It grieves us to the very heart to see such of our Frontier Inhabitants as have escaped Savage Fury with the loss of their parents, their Children, their Wives or Relatives, left destitute by the public, and exposed to the most cruel Poverty and Wretchedness while upwards of an Hundred and twenty of these Savages, who are with great reason suspected of being guilty of these horrid Barbarities, under the Mask of Friendship, have procured themselves to be taken under the protection of the Government, with a view to elude the Fury of the brave Relatives of the murdered, and are now maintained at the public Expence. Some of these Indians now in the Barracks of Philadelphia, are confessedly a part of the Wyalousing Indians, which Tribe is now at War with us, and the others are the Moravian Indians, who, living with us under the Cloak of Friendship, carried on a Correspondence with our known Enemies on the Great Island. We cannot but observe, with sorrow & indignation, that some Persons in this Province are at pains to extenuate the barbarous Cruelties practiced by these Savages on our murdered Brethren & Relatives, which are shocking to human Nature, and must pierce every Heart, but that of the hardened perpetrators or their Abbettors; Nor is it less distressing to hear others pleading that, although the Wyalousing Tribe is at War with us, yet that part of it which is under the Protection of the Government, may be friendly to the English, and innocent. In what nation under the Sun was it ever the custom that when a neighboring Nation took up Arms, not an individual should be touched but only the Persons that offered Hostilities? Who ever proclaimed War with a part of a Nation, and not with the Whole? Had these Indians disapproved of the Perfidy of their Tribe, & been willing to cultivate and preserve Friendship with us, why did they not give notice of the War before it happened, as it is known to be the Result of long Deliberations, and a preconcerted Combination among them? Why did they not leave their Tribe immediately, and come among us before there was Ground to suspect them, or War was actually waged with their Tribe? No, they stayed amongst them, were privy to their murders & Ravages, until we had destroyed their Provisions, and when they could no longer subsist at home, they come, not as Deserters, but as Friends, to be maintained through the Winter, that they may be able to Scalp and butcher us in the Spring.

And as to the Moravian Indians, there are strong Grounds at least to suspect their Friendship, as it is known they carried on a Correspondence with our Enemies on the Great Island. We killed three Indians going from Bethlehem to the Great Island with Blankets, Ammunition, & Provisions, which is an undeniable Proof that the Moravian Indians were in confederacy with our open Enemies; And we cannot but be filled with Indignation to hear this action of ours painted in the most odious and detestable Colors, as if we had inhumanly murdered our Guides, who preserved us from perishing in the Woods, when we only killed three of our known Enemies, who attempted to shoot us when we surprized them. And besides all this, we understand that one of these very Indians is proved by the oath of Stinton's Widow, to be the very Person that murdered her Husband. How then comes it to pass, that he alone, of all the Moravian Indians, should join with the enemy to murder that family? Or can it be supposed that any Enemy Indians, contrary to their known custom of making War, should penetrate into the Heart of a settled Country, to burn, plunder, and murder the Inhabitants, and not molest any Houses in their return, or ever be seen or heard of? Or how can we account for it, that no ravages have been committed in Northampton County, since the removal of the Moravian Indians, when the Great Cove has been struck since? These things put it beyond doubt with us that the Indians now at Philadelphia are His Majesty's Perfidious Enemies, & therefore to protect and maintain them at the Public Expence, while our suffering Brethren on the Frontiers are almost destitute of the necessaries of Life, and are neglected by the Public, is sufficient to make us mad with rage, and tempt us to do what nothing but the most violent necessity can vindicate. We humbly and earnestly pray, therefore, that those Enemies of His Majesty may be removed as soon as possible out of the Province.

Fourthly. We humbly conceive that it is contrary to the maxims of good Policy, and extremely dangerous to our Frontiers, to suffer any Indians, of what tribe soever, to live within the Inhabited parts of this Province, while we are engaged in an Indian War, as Experience has taught us that they are all perfidious, & their Claim to Freedom & Independency, puts it in their power to act as Spies, to entertain & give intelligence to our Enemies, and to furnish them with Provisions and Warlike Stores. To this fatal intercourse, between our pretended Friends and open Enemies, we must ascribe the greatest of the Ravages and Murders that have been committed in the course of this and the last Indian War. We, therefore, pray that this grievance be taken under consideration and remedied.

Fifthly. We cannot help lamenting that no Provision has been hitherto made, that such of our Frontier Inhabitants as have been wounded in defence of the Province, their Lives and Liberties, may be taken care of, and cured of their Wounds at the publick Expence. We, therefore, pray that this Grievance may be redressed.

Sixthly. In the late Indian War this Province, with others of His Majesty's Colonies, gave rewards for Indian Scalps, to encourage the seeking them in their own Country, as the most likely means of destroying or reducing them to reason, but no such Encouragement has been given in this War, which has damped the Spirits of many brave Men, who are willing to venture their Lives in parties against the Enemy. We, therefore, pray that public rewards may be proposed for Indian Scalps, which may be adequate to the Dangers attending Enterprizes of this nature.

Seventhly. We daily lament that numbers of our nearest & dearest relatives are still in Captivity among the Savage Heathen, to be trained up in all their Ignorance & Barbarity, or to be tortured to death with all the contrivances of Indian Cruelty, for attempting to make their escape from Bondage; We see they pay no regard to the many solemn

Promises which they have made to restore our Friends who are in Bondage amongst them. We, therefore, earnestly pray that no trade may hereafter be permitted to be carried on with them, until our Brethren and Relatives are brought home to us.

Eighthly. We complain that a certain Society of People in this Province, in the late Indian War, & at several Treaties held by the King's representatives, openly loaded the Indians with Presents, and that J. P., a leader of the said Society, in Defiance of all Government, not only abetted our Indian Enemies, but kept up a private intelligence with them, and publickly received from them a Belt of Wampum, as if he had been our Governor, or authorized by the King to treat with his Enemies. By this means the Indians have been taught to despise us as a weak and disunited people, and from this fatal Source have arose many of our Calamities under which we groan. We humbly pray, therefore, that this Grievance may be redressed, and that no private subject be hereafter permitted to treat with, or carry on a Correspondence with our Enemies.

Ninthly. We cannot but observe with sorrow, that Fort Augusta, which has been very expensive to this Province, has afforded us but little assistance during this, or the last War. The men that were stationed at that place neither helped our distressed Inhabitants to save their Crops, nor did they attack our Enemies in their Towns, or patrole on our Frontiers. We humbly request that proper measures may be taken to make that Garrison more serviceable to us in our Distress, if it can be done.

N. B. We are far from intending any Reflection against the Commanding Officer stationed at Augusta, as we presume his Conduct was always directed by those from whom he received his Orders.

Signed on Behalf of ourselves, and by appointment of a great number of the Frontier Inhabitants.

MATTHEW SMITH,
JAMES GIBSON,

February 13th, 1764.

B.

THE QUAKERS REPLY

⚶ In an "address" to Governor John Penn, the Quakers defended their actions and refuted charges contained in the *Declaration* and *Remonstrance* that seemed to be directed against them. This Quaker statement of principles was printed in the *Pennsylvania Gazette*. ("The Address of the People called Quakers," *Pennsylvania Gazette*, March 1, 1764.)

How did the Quakers answer the charges made by the frontiersmen?

What was the Quaker attitude toward "Pacification" of the Indians?]

To JOHN PENN, Esq.
Lieutenant Governor of the Province of Pennsylvania, &c.
The ADDRESS of the People called QUAKERS in the said Province.

May it please the GOVERNOR,

WE ACKNOWLEDGE thy kind Reception of our Application for Copies of the two Papers presented to thee by some of the Frontier Inhabitants of this Province, on the 6th and 13th Instant, which we have perused and considered, and find several Parts thereof are evidently intended to render us odious to our Superiors, and to keep up a tumultuous Spirit among the inconsiderate Part of the People.

We therefore request thy favourable Attention to some Observations which we apprehend necessary to offer, to assert our Innocence of the false Charges, and unjust Insinuations, thus invidiously propagated against us.

Our religious Society hath been well known through the British Dominions above an Hundred Years, and was never concerned in promoting or countenancing any Plots or Insurrections against the Government; but on the contrary, when ambitious Men, thirsting for Power, have embroiled the State in intestine Commotions and Bloodshed, subverting the Order of Government, our Forefathers, by their public Declarations, and peaceable Conduct, manifested their Abhorrence of such traiterous Proceedings; and notwithstanding they were often subjected to gross Abuses in their Characters and Persons, and cruel Imprisonments, Persecutions, and some of them to the Loss of their Lives, through the Instigation of wicked and unreasonable Men, they steadily maintained their Profession, and acted agreeable to the Principles of the true Disciples of CHRIST; and by their innocent peaceable Conduct, having approved themselves faithful and loyal Subjects, they obtained the Favour of the Government, and were by Royal Authority entrusted with many valuable Rights and Privileges, to be enjoyed by them and their Successors, with the Property they purchased in the Soil of this Province; which induced them to remove from their native Land, with some of their Neighbours of other religious Societies, and at their own Expence, without any Charge to the Public, to encounter the Difficulties of improving a Wilderness, in which the Blessing of divine Providence attended their Endeavours beyond all human Expectation; and from the first Settling of the Province, till within a few Years past, both the Framing and Administration of the Laws were committed chiefly to Men of our religious Principles, under whom Tranquility and Peace were preserved among the Inhabitants, and with the Natives. The Land rejoiced, and every Man was protected in his Person and Property, and in the full Enjoyment of Religious and Civil Liberty; but with Grief and Sorrow, for some Years past, we have observed the Circumstances of the Province to be much changed, and that intestine Animosities, and the desolating Calamities of War, have taken Place of Tranquility and Peace.

We have, as a religious Society, ever carefully avoided admitting Matters immediately relating to Civil Government into our Deliberations, farther than to excite and engage each other to demean ourselves as dutiful Subjects to the King, with due Respect to those in Authority under him, and to live agreeable to the religious Principles we profess, and to the uniform Example of our Ancestors, and to this End Meetings were instituted, and are still maintained, in which our Care and Concern are manifested to preserve that Discipline and good Order among us, which tend only to the Promotion of Piety and Virtue; yet as Members of Civil Society, Services sometimes occur which we do not judge expedient to become the Subject of the Considerations of our religious Meetings, and of this Nature is the Association formed by a Number of Persons in religious Profession with us, of which on this Occasion it seems incumbent on us to give some Account to the Governor, as their Conduct is misrepresented, in order to calumniate and reproach us as a religious Society, by the Insinuations and Slanders in the Papers sent to the Governor, and particularly in the unsigned Declaration, on Behalf of a Number of armed Men, on the Sixth Instant, then approaching the City, from distant Parts of the Province, to the Disturbance of the public Peace.

In the Spring of the Year 1756, the Distress of the Province being very great, and the desolating Calamities of a general Indian War apprehended, at the Instance of the Provincial Interpreter Conrad Weiser, and with the Approbation of Governor Morris, some of us essayed to promote a Reconciliation with the Indians, and their Endeavours being blessed with Success, the happy Effects thereof were soon manifest, and a real Concern for the then deplorable Situation of our Fellow Subjects on the Frontiers prevailing, in order that they might be capable of rendering some effectual Service; they freely contributed considerable Sums of Money, and engaged others in like Manner to contribute, so that about 5000 £ was raised, in order to be employed for the Service of the Public, and chief Part thereof hath been since expended in Presents given at the public Tréaties (where they were sometimes delivered by the Governors of this Province, and at other times with their Privity and Permission) for promoting the salutary Measures of regaining and confirming Peace with the Indians, and procuring the Release of our Countrymen in Captivity; and thereby a considerable Number have been restored to their Friends; and we find that the Measures thus pursued being made known to the King's Generals, who from time to time were here, and having been communicated by an Address sent to the Proprietaries of this Province in England, appear, by their written Answers, and other Testimonials, to have received their Countenance and Approbation. This being the Case, and the Conduct of those concerned in these Affairs, evidently contrary to the Intent and Tendency of the Assertion contained in the said unsigned Declaration, pretended to be founded on the Records of the County of Berks, we do not apprehend it necessary to say any more thereon, than that we are (after proper Enquiry) assured, that nothing of that Kind is to be found on those Records, and that the private Minute made by Conrad Weiser, of a Report he had received from two Indians, of a Story they had heard from another Indian, pretending to be a Messenger from the Ohio, does not mention any Person whatever, nor contain the Charges expressed in the Declaration, and from the Enquiry we have made, we find them groundless and unjust, and uttered with a View to amuse and inflame the Credulous, and to vilify and calumniate us.

The invidious Reflection against a Sect "that have got the political Reins in their Hands, and tamely tyrannize over the good People of this Province;" though evidently levelled against us, manifests the Authors of these Papers are egregiously ignorant of our Conduct, or wilfully bent on misrepresenting us; it being known that as a religious Body we have, by publick Advices, and private Admonitions, laboured with, and earnestly desired, our Brethren, who have been elected or appointed to public Offices in the Government for some Years past, to decline taking upon them a Task become so arduous, under our late and present Circumstances; and that many have concurred with us in this Resolution is evident, by divers having voluntarily resigned their Seats in the House of Assembly, and by others having, by public Advertisements, signified their declining the Service, and requesting their Countrymen to choose others in their Places, and that many have refused to accept of Places in the executive Part of the Government. We are not conscious that as Englishmen, and dutiful Subjects, we have ever forfeited our Right of electing or being elected; but because we could serve no longer in those Stations with Satisfaction to ourselves, many of us have chosen to forbear the Exercise of these Rights, and wish a Disposition of a contrary Nature was not so manifest in our Adversaries.

The Accusation of our having been profuse to Savages, and carefully avoiding to contribute to the Relief and Support of the distressed Families on the Frontiers, who have abandoned their Possessions, and fled for their Lives, is equally invidious and mistaken; we very early and expeditiously promoted a Subscription, and contributed to the Relief of the Distresses of those who were plundered, and fled from their Habitations in the Beginning of the Indian War, which was distributed among them, in Provisions and Cloathing, and afforded a seasonable Relief. Divers among us, in the City of Philadelphia, also contributed with others the last Summer, and we are well assured that Money was raised, and sent up by the Members of our Society in different Parts of the Country; and as soon as we were informed, that the greatest Part of what had been voluntarily raised by the Citizens of Philadelphia was nearly expended, a Subscription was set on Foot, to which several very generously contributed, and a large Sum might soon have been raised, and was stopped only on Account of the Tumult which hath lately happened; and it hath been from our Regard to our Fellow Subjects on the Frontiers, and Sympathy with their afflicting Distresses, and a Concern for the general Welfare of the Province, that engaged our Brethren to raise the Money they applied to promote a Pacification with the Natives, and no separate Views of Interest to ourselves; but thus unhappily our most upright and disinterested Intentions are misconstrued and perverted, to impose on the Weak, and answer the pernicious Schemes of the Enemies of Peace.

The eighth Paragraph of the second Paper, called the Remonstrance, being chiefly answered by the foregoing Observations, it may be necessary only to observe, on the malicious Charge of "abetting the Indian Enemies, and keeping up a private Intelligence with them," which we can assure the Governor is altogether false and groundless, and we do not know of any Member of our Society chargeable therewith; the Transaction relating to the String (which they have called a Belt of Wampum) we find by Letters from General Forbes, and other Paper produced to us, was in Consequence of a Message sent by the King's Deputy Agent to the Indians on the Ohio, in the name of Sir William Johnson, their Brother Onas, and the Descendants of the first Settlers who came over with their antient Brother William Penn; as also of Frederick Pott's being engaged by some Members of our Community to go on another Message to these Indians, by the express Orders of that General, who then commanded the King's Army, and with the Concurrence of the Governor of this Province; but we do not approve or think it allowable for any private Subject to carry on a Correspondence, or treat with the Enemies of the King and Government, nor to engage in the Transaction of any Affairs of the Government, without the Privity and Consent of those in Authority over us.

We desire the Governor to excuse our taking this Opportunity of exculpating ourselves from another false Accusation, industriously propagated, with a Design to reproach us as a Society; it having been reported, during the late Commotion in this City, that some Persons of our Community had, in the Evening of the 6th Instant, removed, from or near the Barracks, six Indians, to an Island in the River, nearly opposite the City, with a Design to conceal them, and evade their being seen and examined by some of the People from the Frontiers, and that an ex Parte Deposition of an Apprentice Boy was taken to that Purpose; upon hearing which, some of us immediately requested to have the said Boy and his Master carefully examined before the Mayor; in Consequence thereof, both of them were enjoined and required by the Recorder, and one of the Aldermen, to appear before the Mayor, in the Morning of the 11th Inst. at 11 o'Clock; but it appeared, from the Testimony of his Master, that before the Time appointed the Boy absconded, and after diligent Search is not since found. Wherefore the Mayor, after the Examination of the Military Officers (to whose Care the Indians had been committed) and of other Witnesses relating to the Matter, upon considering thereof, and the Circumstances attending the Relation; first the Alderman, before whom the Deposition had been made, and afterwards the Mayor publickly declared, they were convinced the Accusation was utterly false and groundless.

It would be a tedious Task for us to undertake to answer all the slanderous Reports, and Misrepresentations, which have been spread, with a Design to prejudice our Characters, through the Malice of some, and the Ignorance of others; but having the Testimony of our Consciences to recur to for our Innocence, we hope, through Divine Assistance, we shall be enabled to bear Reproaches; and, by the

Uprightness of our Conduct, shew forth to the World, that we live in the Fear of GOD, and pay the just Returns of dutiful Submission to the King, for the Continuance of his paternal Tenderness towards us; and that we are, as we have ever been, real Friends to the Government, and steadily desirous of acting agreeable to our Stations, as Members of Civil Society.

Signed on Behalf, and by Order of a Committee appointed to represent our Religious Society in Pennsylvania and New-Jersey, at a Meeting held in Philadelphia, the 25th of Second-Month, 1764.
SAMUEL EMLEN, junior, Clerk.

C.

THE WAR OF PAMPHLETS

❡1. *Franklin's A Narrative of the Late Massacres.* Soon after the Lancaster massacre a number of pamphlets appeared putting forward the views of the Quaker party or of their opponents, the frontiersmen. Many of these pamphlets produced more heat than light. Even Franklin's pro-Quaker *Narrative*, accusing the Paxton Boys of cowardice, was acknowledged by its author to be a political tract—which is another way of saying that it was directed more toward the emotions of the readers than toward their reason. ([Benjamin Franklin], *A Narrative of the Late Massacres, in Lancaster County, of a Number of Indians, Friends of this Province, by Persons Unknown, With Some Observations on the Same* [Philadelphia], 1764.)

What accusations did Franklin make?

How did Franklin appeal to the reader's emotions?]

. . . . O YE unhappy Perpetrators of this horrid Wickedness! Reflect a Moment on the Mischief ye have done, the Disgrace ye have brought on your Country, on your Religion, and your Bible, on your Families and Children! Think on the Destruction of your captivated Country-folks (now among the wild *Indians*) which probably may follow, in Resentment of your Barbarity! Think on the Wrath of the United *Five Nations*, hitherto our Friends, but now provoked by your murdering one of their Tribes, in Danger of becoming our bitter Enemies.—Think of the mild and good Government you have so audaciously insulted; the Laws of your King, your Country, and your GOD, that you have broken; the infamous Death that hangs over your Heads:—For JUSTICE, though slow, will come at last.—All good People every where detest your Actions.—You have imbrued your Hands in innocent Blood; how will you make them clean?—The dying Shrieks and Groans of the Murdered, will often sound in your Ears: Their Spectres will sometimes attend you, and affright even your innocent Children!—Fly where you will, your Consciences will go with you:—Talking in your Sleep shall betray you, in the Delirium of a Fever you yourselves shall make your own Wickedness known.

One Hundred and Forty peaceable *Indians* yet remain in the

Government. They have, by Christian Missionaries, been brought over to a *Liking* at least, of our Religion; some of them lately left their Nation which is now at War with us, because they did not chuse to join with them in their Depredations; and to shew their Confidence in us, and to give us an equal Confidence in them, they have brought and put into our Hands their Wives and Children. Others have lived long among us in *Northampton* County, and most of their Children have been born there. These are all now trembling for their Lives. They have been hurried from Place to Place for Safety, now concealed in Corners, then sent out of the Province, refused a Passage through a neighbouring Colony, and returned, not unkindly perhaps, but disgracefully, on our Hands. O *Pennsylvania!* once renowned for Kindness to Strangers, shall the Clamours of a few mean Niggards about the Expence of the *Publick Hospitality*, an Expence that will not cost the noisy Wretches *Six-pence* a Piece (and what is the Expence of the poor Maintenance we afford them, compared to the Expence that might occasion if in Arms against us) shall so senseless a Clamour, I say, force you to turn out of your Doors these unhappy Guests, who have offended their own Country-folks by their Affection for you, who, confiding in your Goodness, have put themselves under your Protection? Those whom you have disarmed to satisfy groundless Suspicions, will you leave them exposed to the armed Madmen of your Country?—Unmanly Men! who are not ashamed to come with Weapons against the Unarmed, to use the Sword against Women, and the Bayonet against young Children; and who have already given such bloody Proofs of their Inhumanity and Cruelty.—Let us rouze ourselves, for Shame, and redeem the Honour of our Province from the Contempt of its Neighbours; let all good Men join heartily and unanimously in Support of the Laws, and in strengthening the Hands of Government; that JUSTICE may be done, the Wicked punished, and the Innocent protected; otherwise we can, as a People, expect no Blessing from Heaven, there will be no Security for our Persons or Properties; Anarchy and Confusion will prevail over all, and Violence, without Judgment, dispose of every Thing.

When I mention the Baseness of the Murderers, in the Use they made of Arms, I cannot, I ought not to forget, the very different Behaviour of *brave Men* and *true Soldiers,* of which this melancholy Occasion has afforded us fresh Instances. The *Royal Highlanders* have, in the Course of this War, suffered as much as any other Corps, and have frequently had their Ranks thinn'd by an *Indian* Enemy; yet they did not for this retain a brutal undistinguishing Resentment against *all Indians,* Friends as well as Foes. But a Company of them happening to be here, when the 140 poor *Indians* above mentioned were thought in too much Danger to stay longer in the Province, chearfully undertook to protect and escort them to *New-York,* which they executed (as far as that Government would permit the *Indians* to come) with Fidelity and Honour; and their Captain *Robinson,* is justly applauded and honoured by all sensible and good People, for the Care, Tenderness and Humanity, with which he treated those

unhappy Fugitives, during their March in this severe Season. General *Gage*, too, has approved of his Officer's Conduct, and, as I hear, ordered him to remain with the *Indians* at *Amboy*, and continue his Protection to them, till another Body of the King's Forces could be sent to relieve his Company, and escort their Charge back in Safety to *Philadelphia*, where his Excellency has had the Goodness to direct those Forces to remain for some Time, under the Orders of our Governor, for the Security of the *Indians*; the Troops of this Province being at present necessarily posted on the Frontier. Such just and generous Actions endear the Military to the Civil Power, and impress the Minds of all the Discerning with a still greater Respect for our national Government.—I shall conclude with observing, that *Cowards* can handle Arms, can strike where they are sure to meet with no Return, can wound, mangle and murder; but it belongs to *brave* Men to spare, and to protect; for, as the Poet says,
—*Mercy still sways the Brave*

[2. *Hugh Williamson, The Plain Dealer, A Pro-Frontier Pamphlet.* In the following pamphlet the Quakers are accused of corruption and inefficiency, of passing unjust laws in the assembly, and of inciting Indian attack. (Hugh Williamson, *The Plain Dealer* [Philadelphia, 1764], No. I.)
What specific accusations were made against the Quakers?
What were said to be the Quaker motives?]

FOR SEVERAL years I have been a silent spectator of the political conduct of a particular faction in this province; I have observ'd how they have ruled in most public transactions; have handled the public money, and disposed of our lives and fortunes at pleasure: I have seen this very faction raise the hue and cry about liberty, while they were stealing the poor remains of liberty from the miserable inhabitants of the province: And I have now observ'd that while the injur'd and distressed are crying for redress, they are endeavouring to plunge us into new schemes, in order to amuse us; tho' the wound is still bleeding of which we have complain'd. In such a situation, silence would no longer become a friend of liberty and his country. And as our representatives are gone home to consult with their constituents, what is to be done in this conjuncture, I think we are now in a particular manner call'd upon to speak out, and tell what we take to be the origin of all our troubles, and what is the best way to cure them. For my part, I am clearly persuaded that Quaker politicks, and a Quaker faction, have involv'd this province into almost all the contentions, and all the miseries under which we have so long struggled.

There can never be a greater cause, perhaps no other cause of tumults and complaints in any government, than the people conceiving that unjust laws are imposed on them, and that measures are pursued to which they did not consent. This is the very case with the majority of this province. They are depriv'd of their share in legislation; laws are made and impos'd on them, and measures are taken which they do not approve, and yet cannot prevent, because they are not fairly represented in Assembly. This would be in any view, an intolerable grievance, as it deprives us of liberty; but that grievance is doubled, when we consider that it is contrary to an express stipulation in Charter, for which we left our native country, and came to this howling wilderness.—This grievance is the foundation of all our trouble, and has its origin from Quakers. You, Gentlemen, soon perceiv'd that the majority of your people were come over at first, and that all future increase of this province would be of other denominations. The government was in your hands, and that you might never loose it, you resolv'd to deprive all new Counties of their rights as Englishmen, and their rights by the Proprietor's charter: And you have so contrived it, that three Quaker counties may give laws to all the province, altho' it should contain fifteen counties. If you had not form'd new counties, the people now in those counties must have voted amongst you, and might have turn'd you out of power; but now you have made blanks of them for ever; and by this scheme they must ever wear such a yoke as a Quaker may please to shape for them. If the province is to be protected, the principal of Non-Resistance takes place, and we must protect your lives; but if money is to be rais'd, a very different principal takes place, and you will take care of our money. In this blessed situation we have jogg'd on, and call'd our selves Freemen. This poor sun-burned African comes to a more desirable slavery in this province than we; for his master is at least careful of his life; but ours diligently pursue such practices as bring us to destruction.

In the beginning of the last French war, you would not grant so much as £10,000 for his Majesty's service; you had not started your quarrel with the Proprietor then, but you plead conscience, and that did as well. On account of such conduct the English parliament had like to've turn'd you out of the Assembly for ever; but your Friends in London interceded, and come over to persuade you to resign; and resign you did with great reluctance, just so as to make a sham majority of other denominations in the House: But some of the gentlemen that you chose would not go heartily into your measures, so you turned them out, and have put a great majority of Quakers in the Assembly again. However tho', with much trouble his Majesty obtained supplies; yet, like good engineers, you found a way to counter-plot him. It may not indeed become us who are slaves, to say this; but we may tell you, that his Majesty's General, his Governor, and his Agent for Indian affairs, have said that you *invaded the King's prerogative royal*, and *presume to treat with foreign princes*, with whom we are at war; and *act as moderators between the government and an independant people*. From this conduct have flow'd those streams of innocent blood with which our frontiers have been drench'd for many years. Soon as war was proclaim'd with the Indians, you opened a correspondence with them, you created a King among them, and him you supported for several years as your Deputy-Enemy to the Proprietor, and the poor inhabitants of our frontiers. You taught him to accuse the Proprietor. The Indians also say, and we have much reason to believe it, that you persuaded them to kill the frontier inhabitants. It is certain, however, that you falsly persuaded them that they were cheated; and that was the proper way to make them kill the people: You attended at public treaties; procured a secretary of state for your Indian King, and furnish'd him with whatever was necessary for his purposes and your's. When the Governor complain'd of this treasonable tampering and treating with Indians, you modestly told him that you would do it whether he was pleas'd with it or not; for you did not chuse to leave the Governor and King's agent to manage the business without you. We need not tell what blood this has cost our province: The miserable Dutch and Irish on the frontiers have felt your scourge, and the groans of many a thousand widows and fatherless children which daily pierce the heavens, will tell it, as far as the Quaker-government in Pennsylvania shall be known.

In order yet to prove that you have abus'd the province, need I mention how the public money has been squandered away? You rais'd large sums, but always granted them too late, as tho' on purpose that little might be done. Was ever half a million of money so consumed as it has been in this province? It was not with our many troops; for a New-England colony has rais'd three times the number of troops, and yet never spent such sums of money. Does any man ask what is become of this money? Many a thousand pounds were spent in debating with the Governor about things that you knew he could not grant; many thousands as bribes to G——r D——, to obtain iniquitous laws, and to pervert justice; many a thousand to support your friends, in order to maintain your faction; many a thousand to murtherers, and his Majesty's enemies; and a great many thousands where Quakers alone can tell, tho' it may not suit them to tell: But hardly ever was a farthing given to support the naked and perishing frontier inhabitants; to whom the Indians that you fed, had left nothing but the miserable life. And in this present Indian war, it is notorious, that great sums of money were spent last summer, while the most effectual endeavours were used to order matters so as to render no effectual service to the poor and defenceless inhabitants. It is no wonder, as a Prime Minister lately informed us, that "His Majesty sees through such artifices."

In this manner you have tyranniz'd over the good people on the frontiers of this province.—If you might avail your selves of a friendship and trade with the Indians, no matter what miseries we suffer'd; if you might help the Indians to recover their lands from the Proprietor, no matter what became of the people who lived on those lands: And suffer me to observe, this conduct of yours, and not the price of lands, was the true cause of thousands leaving this province. The Scots and Irish were rode by main force; and the unhappy Germans, being ignorant of our constitution, have been blindly led into your schemes, and patiently groan'd under the burthen, while their wives, their children, and all were perishing by fire and hatchet.

But when you find that the province is to be enslav'd no longer; the frontier counties, almost to a man, insist on having justice done them; the Hibernian winches beneath his yoke; the German, having lost every thing else, begins to pray that you would spare his life:—In short, the voice of misery and distress is no longer to be stifled. . . .

III

EFFECTS AND ASSESSMENTS

ALL THE MARCHING AND BUTCHERY DID LITTLE TO IMPROVE THE SITUATION of the frontiersmen. True, slight concessions were conceded by the assembly: a bounty for Indian scalps was approved and additional troops were provided for frontier defense. But those in power were reluctant to give way to the land squatter on the frontier and to the discontented easterner who might share his grievances. The government was not, however, able to apprehend those responsible for the massacres; popular opposition proved too strong.

Perhaps the most important result of the riots was that they showed the pioneers that they could depend upon some sympathy from the East—a sympathy which proved to be extremely important in 1776 in helping to bring about the passage of a bill for reapportionment in the assembly.

A.

EFFECTS

❡ 1. *An Indian Scalp Bounty.* As a result of a formidable Indian attack on the frontier in 1763-64, during Pontiac's uprising, Governor John Penn issued a proclamation of war against the Delaware and Shawanese Indians on July 7, 1764. Part of the proclamation (quoted here) included a reward for Indian scalps, which had been the sixth demand in the *Remonstrance.* (George Edward Reed, ed., *Pennsylvania Archives,* Fourth Series [Harrisburg, Pennsylvania, 1900], III, 292-93.)

What different kinds of "premiums and Bounties" were offered? Why was a larger reward offered for prisoners than for scalps?]

. . . . WHEREAS, IT is necessary for the better carrying on Offensive Operations against our Indian Enemies, and bringing the unhappy war with them to a speedy issue, that the greatest Encouragements should be given to all his Majesty's Subjects to exert and use their utmost Endeavours to pursue, attack, take, and destroy our said Enemy Indians, I do hereby declare and promise, that there shall be paid out of the Monies lately granted for his Majesty's use, to all and every Person and persons not in the pay of this Province, the following several and respective premiums and Bounties for the prisoners and Scalps of the Enemy Indians that shall be taken or killed within the Bounds of this Province, as limited by the Royal Charter, or in pursuit from within the said Bounds, that is to say: For every Male Indian Enemy above ten Years old, who shall be taken Prisoner, and delivered at any Forts garrisoned by the Troops in the pay of this Province, or at any of the County Towns, to the Keeper of the Common Gaols there, the sum of One hundred & fifty Spanish Dollars, or pieces of Eight; For every Female Indian Enemy taken Prisoner, & brought in as aforesaid, and for every Male Indian Enemy of ten years old, or under, taken Prisoner, and delivered as aforesaid, the sum of One hundred and thirty pieces of Eight; For the Scalp of every Male Indian Enemy above the age of ten years, produced as Evidence of their being killed, the sum of One hundred and thirty-four pieces of Eight; and for the Scalp of every Female Indian Enemy above the age of ten Years, produced as Evidence of their being killed, the sum of Fifty pieces of Eight; And that there shall be paid to every Officer or Officers, Soldier or Soldiers, as are or shall be in the pay of this Province, who shall take, bring in, and produce any Indian Enemy Prisoner, or Scalp, as aforesaid, one-half of the said several and respective Premiums & Bounties. . . .

[2. *Reapportionment in the Pennsylvania Assembly, 1776.* The most important grievance in the *Remonstrance* was that the frontier counties were not properly represented in the assembly. On March 23, 1776, only a few months before the Declaration of Independence, the assembly approved an act (the text of which follows) for bringing about a reapportionment. Some twelve years after the Paxton riots the demand of the frontiersmen that they be fairly represented in the assembly of the state was granted legislative recognition. (*Pennsylvania Gazette*, March 27, 1776.)

How was the act justified?

Which of the frontier counties mentioned in the *Remonstrance* were to elect assembly representatives?]

PHILADELPHIA, March 27.
An ACT to encrease the Number of Representatives in Assembly for the City of Philadelphia, *and in the several Counties therein named.*

WHEREAS IT is essential to the good Government of every free state, that all its component Parts should have a just and adequate Share in the Legislature. AND WHEREAS the City of *Philadelphia,* and the several Counties herein after particularly named, have not at this Time such Share in the Legislature of this Province: For Remedy whereof, BE IT ENACTED by the Honourable *JOHN PENN*, Esq; Governor and Commander in Chief of the Province of *Pennsylvania*, by and with the Consent and Advice of the Representatives of the Freemen of the said Province, in General Assembly met, and by the Authority of the same, That the Freeholders and Inhabitants of the respective Wards, Townships and Districts, in the said City and Counties respectively, qualified by the Laws of this Province to elect Members of Assembly, shall meet at some convenient Place within their respective Townships, Wards and Districts, on the Twenty-fifth Day of *April* next, and proceed to choose Inspectors, as is directed by the Laws of this Province in such Cities, having had due and legal Notice of such Meeting by the Person or Persons appointed by Law for that Purpose, which they are hereby enjoined and required to give, under the same Pains and Penalties as are inflicted for Neglect of Duty in the like Cases by Law. And that the Freeholders and Inhabitants of the said City of *Philadelphia*, and the Freeholders and Inhabitants of the Counties of *Lancaster, York, Cumberland, Berks, Northampton, Bedford, Northumberland* and *Westmoreland*, respectively, qualified by the Charter and Laws of this Province to vote at the General Elections for said City and Counties respectively, shall, on the First Day of *May* next, meet in the said City and Counties respectively, at the usual Places for holding General Elections in the said City and Counties respectively, and elect an additional Number of Burgesses, Representatives or Delegates, to serve them in General Assembly; for the City of *Philadelphia* Four, for the County of *Lancaster* Two, for the County of *York* Two, for the County of *Cumberland* Two, for the County of *Berks* Two, for the County of *Northampton* Two, for the County of *Bedford* One, for the County of *Northumberland* One, and for the County of *Westmoreland* One, in the same Manner as by the Charter and Laws of this Province is directed in respect to the Choice of other Members for the said City and Counties respectively; which said Burgesses, Representatives or Delegates, so chosen, and returned as the Laws of this Province in such Cases direct, shall be Members of the General Assembly of this Province of *Pennsylvania*, and sit and act as such, as fully and freely as any of the Burgesses or Representatives for the said City and Counties respectively, or the other Counties within this Province, do, may, can, or ought to do.

And be it further enacted, That on the Day following the holding the General Election for the County of *Philadelphia* yearly, for ever hereafter, unless it happen on *Sunday*, and then the Day after, the Freeholders and Inhabitants of the said City, qualified as aforesaid, shall meet at the State-House in the said City, and elect for the said City Six Burgesses, Representatives or Delegates, to serve them in Assembly: And that the Freeholders and Inhabitants of the said Counties of *Lancaster, York, Cumberland, Berks, Northampton, Bedford, Northumberland* and *Westmoreland*, shall meet on the First Day of *October* next, and yearly for ever hereafter, unless it happen on a *Sunday*, and then the Day following, at the Court-Houses in the said respective Counties, where Court-Houses are already erected, and in such Counties as have not erected Court-Houses, then, until Court-Houses shall be built, at the Places where General Elections for such Counties have been usually held, and elect for the County of *Lancaster* Six, for the County of *York* Four, for the County of *Cumberland* Four, for the County of *Berks* Four, for the County of *Northampton* Four, for the County of *Bedford* Two, for the County of *Northumberland* Two, and for the County of *Westmoreland* Two Representatives or Delegates, to serve them in Assembly, in the same Manner as by the Charter and Laws of this Province is directed in respect to the Representatives or Delegates of the other Counties of this Province; which said Representatives, when so chosen in the said City and respective Counties aforesaid, shall be Members of the General Assembly of this Province of *Pennsylvania*, and shall sit and act as such, as fully and freely as any of the Representatives for the other Counties within this province do, may, can, or ought to do.

And be it further enacted, That Notice shall be given in Writing, and shall be proclaimed in the most public Places of the said City, and of the capital Town or Place where such Election is to be, of the Time and Place of such Election, by the Sheriffs of the Counties respectively; and the said Sheriffs shall cause Copies of such Notice or Advertisement to be posted upon some House, in the Way leading from every Township or Precinct to the Town or Place where the said Election is to be, as also upon the Court-Houses and most public Places in every Township in the said respective Counties, at least Fifteen Days before the Time of such Election.

And be it further enacted by the Authority aforesaid, That so much of the several Acts of General Assembly of this Province, as relates to the allowing the said City, and the several and respective Counties aforesaid, a less Number of Representatives or Delegates, to serve in General Assembly for the said City and Counties respectively, than is hereby directed, shall be, and is hereby declared to be, repealed.

Provided nevertheless, That the Members of Assembly already chosen under the same, shall be and continue to act until the First Day of *October* next, as fully and freely as if this Act had never been made.

Passed March 23, 1776.

B.

ASSESSMENTS

¶ 1. *A Quaker Letter, February 29, 1764.* The following anonymous letter was printed in 1833 in *Hazard's Register of Pennsylvania*, a publication devoted to local history. It was made available to this periodical by a subscriber who found it "among some old family papers." Despite its 1764 date, this letter may have been composed after the turmoil caused by the Paxton riots had died down, for it gives an unemotional, factual account of the events. (Samuel Hazard, ed., *Hazard's Register of Pennsylvania* [Philadelphia, July 6, 1833], XII, No. 1, 9-13.)

Why did some Philadelphians approve of the frontier plan to kill Indians sheltered by the city?

How did the frontiersmen justify their march on the city?

What factors caused distrust and animosity between East and West?]

PHILADELPHIA, February 29th, 1764.

OLD FRIEND,—When I last wrote, I did not intend to take up the pen again till I should hear from thee, but an event has happened of so extraordinary a nature, and which at present makes so great a noise here, that I thought a particular relation of it, might not be unacceptable. I am convinced you will have various accounts concerning the matter, some favourable to one side, and some to the other; therefore, I shall endeavour, as far as lies in my power, to give as exact a representation of the whole affair, as possible.

In my last, I informed thee, that a number of Indians had been brought down from the Moravian settlement upon our frontier, and placed by the Government upon the Province Island, where they were to remain till a peace could be effected with those Indians that were then at war with us, or till such time as we were able to subdue them; it is true some persons belonging to this tribe were suspected of being concerned in the murder of the inhabitants, but as no sufficient proof appeared, and as some of them were known to be well affected, and had done us confidential services, it was judged not only just, but likewise consistent with the maxims of prudence and good policy, to invite them down, and take them under our protection; especially as they had requested it, and voluntarily offered to deliver up their arms, as a security for their good behaviour, and a testimony of their having no ill intentions against us.

Besides this tribe, there was another, consisting of about twenty persons, men, women and children, who have lived for many years upon a small tract of land granted to them by the proprietors, in the manor of Conestogo. These poor natives, from their peaceable and quiet behaviour, (having never been concerned in any hostilities against us) were looked upon by the legislature as proper objects of their regard, and were accordingly taken under their protection as well as the others; but with this difference, that they were suffered to remain in their own habitations, where, as they were not allowed the liberty of hunting, they spent their time in making of baskets and brooms, which they sold to the white people for a subsistence.

Whilst these precautions were taking here, in order to prevent the innocent from falling with the guilty, Sir William Johnson was employed on the frontiers of New York, in conciliating the affections of the six nations, who for some unknown cause, appeared to be wavering with respect to the part they should act on the present occasion. It seems by the accounts we have received, that Sir William's negotiation was likely to be attended with all the success that could be wished, five of the confederated tribes seemed sincerely desirous of renewing their ancient friendship and part of the Senecas (the only tribe actually in arms) had been brought over by showing them how inconsistent their conduct was with the dictates of good policy, as the English were now possessed of almost all North America; these, together with others of different nations, engaged to pursuade or compel the remaining part to sue for peace. Indeed Indian affairs in general wore a favourable aspect; our back settlements had not been disturbed, nor had any murders been committed from the month of October; all was calm and quiet, and the conversation of the people in general, began to turn upon other subjects—but in the month of January, part of the inhabitants of Paxton township, together with others from the west side of Susquehanna, who had lost, or pretended to have lost, some of their friends and relations by the Indians, took it into their heads (as they had been out upon several scouts, in which they had destroyed some wigwams, and a few acres of Indian corn without killing any enemies,) that they would attack the Indians upon the manor of Conestogo; accordingly one morning about day break, they came upon this village, and with the most savage fury, destroyed every person in it. Luckily the greatest part of them happened to be abroad, and so soon as they heard of it, flew to the town of Lancaster, where they were received in the most friendly manner, consoled for their losses, and in order to secure them against any further danger, put into the work house. This being done, the Sheriff and several others were sent out to bury the dead, who, when they arrived at the place, found the bodies most shockingly mangled, and the houses burnt to the ground. The heroes who had performed this exploit immediately dispersed themselves; part of them were met by Tommy Wright, who suspecting what they had been about, told them he had supposed they had just returned from killing the Indians upon the manor? They replied, what if they had? Why, says he, if you have, you have done a very base action, for they were under the protection of the government. No government, answered they, has a right to protect heathen. Joshua was ordered to drive the heathen out of the land. Do you believe the scripture? If you do not, we have nothing to say to you, and so left him. I mention this short conversation to give thee an idea of the principles of those who were engaged in this holy war, and who were determined to fulfil the command given to Joshua with the most scrupulous exactness.

Scarce had they time to give thanks for this signal victory, but down they came again in a considerable body, part of them, supposed to be about fifty, entered the town of Lancaster, well armed, rode up to Slough's tavern, turned their horses into the yard, asked where the Indians were, ran to the work house, demanded the keys of the keeper with threats, opened the door, and almost in an instant, shot and toma-hawked every one of them. Neither the mother nor the tender infant that hung at the breast, was spared, though on her knees she begged for mercy, all were alike the objects of their ruthless vengeance, which being satisfied for the present, they returned to their horses and rode off.

Whether this butchery could have been prevented, I cannot take upon myself to determine. There was at the time a company of Highlanders in the town, and it is said, the officer who commanded them put himself in the way of the magistrates, in expectation of receiving orders for that purpose. On the other hand, they say, it was but twelve minutes from the time the Paxtoneers entered the town, till all was over, in which case, considering the general consternation, it seemed too late to make any opposition. Expresses, however, were dispatched to this city, informing us of what had happened, and at the same time, letting us know that a large body of them intended to come down and destroy the Indians upon the Island. Many of the inhabitants were greatly alarmed at this intelligence, and orders were given to provide a number of flats to be ready at the Island, to carry off the Indians into the Jerseys, in case any attempt of that sort should be made. A correspondence was also settled with several persons of note, in different parts of the province, who engaged to give the speediest notice of the motions of these "children of Promise or Saints Militant." In the mean time the Highlanders being arrived here on their way to New York, in order to embark for their native country, it was thought proper, in order to quiet the minds of the people, and to prevent the government from being insulted to send the Indians under their care to that city, from whence they were to proceed to Sir William Johnson, to be disposed of as he should judge most for the interest of the Colonies. But, as the wisest men, and the greatest politicians, are sometimes liable to mistakes, it so happened, that no request was made to the Governor of York to grant them a passage through his territories. Accordingly, when they came to Elizabethtown or Amboy, they received his orders to proceed no further, for that he would not receive them. Their directors were now at a loss what to do, to send them forward they could not, to bring them back was dangerous—in this state of suspense they remained not long, for General Gage interposed in their behalf, and ordered Captain Schlosser with upwards of a hundred Royal Americans to conduct the Indians back to Philadelphia, and guard them till the spring. The Captain accordingly brought them back again, and lodged them in the barracks, that they might be more immediately under the care of the soldiery, and more readily assisted than they could possibly be if they were sent down to the Island.

Whilst they were upon their march through the Jerseys, faction and clamour seemed to subside, but no sooner was it known that they were returned, than the spirit of discord began to operate afresh. At first, only a little murmering was heard, then they began to threaten, so that it became dangerous for a person in any of the back counties to speak his mind with freedom. Nay, so far did they proceed, that letters to and from this city to Lancaster, were obliged to be sent (it is said) unsubscribed, for a practice was made of opening them, and communicating their contents to the disaffected. At last, on the fourth of this month, we received certain intelligence that a considerable body of them were coming down with arms to destroy every Indian they could meet with. The Governor immediately upon this, ordered the

Sheriff and his officers to summon the inhabitants to meet in the afternoon at the State House. A vast concourse accordingly assembled, when it was proposed that they should enter into an association to defend the government, for it was imagined that killing the Indians, was not the only motive of this hostile insurrection. Several persons entered their names directly, and notwithstanding it rained heavily, went and equipped themselves with the implements of war and marched up to the barracks, where they continued under arms with the soldiers all night. Our old friend, the Parson, and a few more belonging to the same peaceable society, were of the number. The Governor was also there with several other gentlemen.

In the morning the weather proving fair, (though very cold) a number of carpenters were hired, who, by Captain Schlosser's direction, build a redoubt, in the centre of the parade, at the barracks, and fortified the gateways with angles of thick plank, which had spaces left between for the soldiers to fire through. Several pieces of cannon were likewise hauled up and the best preparations were made that the time would admit of.

Notwithstanding these warlike measures, the government was still unwilling to proceed to extremity. They thought it best to try the milder methods of pursuasion first, and therefore sent the Reverend G——t T——t with two or three more pious divines of the same order, to convince them if possible, by the force of reason and argument, or by the apposition of texts of scripture, that they were in error, and to prevail upon them to return home. Perhaps some people may be inclined to censure this step, when they consider that a proclamation had been published, offering a reward of two hundred pounds for apprehending any of the parties concerned in the murder of the Indians at Lancaster, and that the riot act had been extended to this province a few days before.

The day passing over, and no enemy appearing, nor any intelligence of their motions, we began to hope that the rumor was without foundation. For my own part I went to bed as free from any apprehensions of danger as ever I did in my life, and slept very soundly till after midnight, when all of a sudden I was alarmed by the ringing of the bells. I listened to know the cause, (being loath to get out of bed as I had a bad cold) expecting it was fire, but no cry, no rattling of engines was to be heard; I then laid myself down with a resolution to go to sleep again, when one of the neighbours thundered at the door, and called to us to put out the lights for the Paxton Boys were coming. Up I jumped immediately, whipped on my clothes, and ran to the door, which I had no sooner opened, than I heard the old militia drums with solemn dubb beating to arms, and saw the inhabitants running from all quarters to obey the summons. By sunrise they had got themselves officers, and brought forth those ensigns which were once displayed with such terror in the glorious battle of the New Market. The remains of the old artillery company were likewise mustered, and two pieces of cannon brought out of the magazine and stationed before the court house. All business was now suspended, the shops and stores were close shut, and every person seemed anxious to know what would be the issue of all this tumult.

Before I proceed further it may not be amiss to inform thee that a great number of the inhabitants here approved of killing the Indians, and declared that they would not offer to oppose the Paxtoneers, unless they attacked the citizens, that is to say, themselves—for, if any judgment was to be formed from countenances and behaviour, those who depended upon them for defence and protection, would have found their confidence shockingly misplaced.

The number of persons in arms that morning was about six hundred, and as it was expected the insurgents would attempt to cross at the middle or upper ferry, orders were sent to bring the boats to this side, and to take away the ropes. Couriers were now seen continually coming in, their horses all of a foam, and people running with the greatest eagerness to ask them where the enemy were, and what were their numbers. The answers to these questions were various, sometimes they were at a distance, then near at hand—sometimes they were a thousand strong, then five hundred, then fifteen hundred; in short, all was doubt and uncertainty.

About eleven o'clock it was recollected the boat at the Sweed's ford was not secured, which, in the present case, was of the utmost consequence; for, as there was a considerable freshet in the Schuylkill, the securing that boat would oblige them to march some distance up the river, and thereby retard the execution of their scheme at least a day or two longer. Several persons therefore set off immediately to get it performed; but they had not been gone long, before there was a general uproar—they are coming! they are coming! Where? Where? down Second street! down Second street! Such of the company as had grounded their fire-locks, flew to arms, and began to prime; the artillery-men threw themselves into order, and the people ran to get out of the way, for a troop of armed men, on horseback, appeared in reality coming down the street, and one of the artillery-men was just going to apply the fatal match, when a person, perceiving the mistake, clapped his hat upon the touch hole of the piece he was going to fire. Dreadful would have been the consequence, had the cannon discharged; for the men that appeared, proved to be a company of German butchers and porters, under the command of Captain Hoffman. They had just collected themselves, and being unsuspicious of danger, had neglected to give notice of their coming;—a false alarm was now called out, and all became quiet again in a few minutes.

In the afternoon we received intelligence that those who were sent to the Sweed's ford, arrived too late, for the Paxtoneers had actually crossed the river, and were got as far as Germantown, where they proposed to take up their quarters for the night. Several persons went from town to view them, and from the best accounts that could be obtained, their numbers did not exceed two hundred; but they pretended that the whole were not come in. This formidable body of forces consisted principally of a set of fellows, dressed in blanket coats and mocassins, like our Indian traders, or back-country wagoners: they were armed with rifles and tomahawks, and some of them had a brace of pistols besides. Few of them were men of any property, but had been hired or persuaded to the undertaking, by persons, whose views and designs may, perhaps, in time, be disclosed, although at present we can only guess at them. Their chiefs were almost as obscure as themselves, but on this occasion, assumed an air of command and importance, (one of them was called Smith, another Gibson, the third I have forgot.) They behaved with great civility to those they conversed with—were surprised to hear that the citizens had taken up arms to oppose them—declared that they had no intention of injuring any one, and only wanted satisfaction of the Indians, as some of them had been concerned in the murder of their friends and relations. All this was very well, with respect to us, but it is much to be doubted, if they would have carried their complaisance so far, had not preparations been made to receive them.

Night now coming on, the inhabitants were dismissed, but ordered to hold themselves in readiness on the first notice;—at break of day the alarm bells rang again and all got under arms.

I should have mentioned that when it was known they were at Germantown, it was proposed in Council to go and take them prisoners, but that advice was overruled. Though Captain Torbet Francis, of the 44th Regiment, (who, at the request of a number of young persons, had undertaken to command them) voluntarily offered to make the attempt; but as it was reported they were excellent marksmen, and as a great deal of blood might probably be spilt upon the occasion, it was resolved to send a body of select patricians to inquire into the object of their coming, and to persuade them to return home; they accordingly set out early in the morning, some of them with great reluctance, as it was a measure they by no means approved of.

The weather being now very wet, Capt. Francis, Capt. Wood and Capt. Mifflin, drew up their men under the market house, which, not affording shelter for any more, they occupied Friends' meeting house, and Capt. Joseph Wharton marched his company upstairs, into the monthly meeting room, as I have been told—the rest were stationed below. It happened to be the day appointed for holding of Youths' Meeting, but never did the Quaker youth assemble in such a military manner—never was the sound of the drum heard before within those walls, nor ever till now was the Banner of War displayed in that rostrum from whence the art has been so zealously declaimed against. Strange reverse of times, James—. Nothing of any consequence passed, during the remainder of the day, except that Captain Coultas came into town at the head of a troop, which he had just raised in his own neighborhood. The Captain was one of those who had been marked out as victims by these devout conquerors; and word was sent to him from Lancaster to make his peace with Heaven, for that he had but about ten days to live.

In the evening our Negotiators came in from Germantown. They had conferred with the Chiefs of this illustrious—, and have prevailed with them to suspend all hostility till such time as they should receive an answer to their petition or manifesto, which had been sent down the day before. This paper was supposed to have been drawn up for them in Philadelphia, in order to colour over their proceedings, and give them an appearance of rectitude; it contained an account of the distressed condition of the back inhabitants, and demanded a release from taxes for a twelvemonth—also, that five or six of the Indians should be brought to trial as murderers, and that the number of representatives for the frontier counties should be increased. As it was necessary that these requisitions should be laid before the Governor and Assembly, the Chiefs agreed to disband their troops and come to town with the Envoys, to enforce them, being promised protection on the faith of the Government.

The weather now clearing, the City forces drew up near the Court House, where a speech was made to them, informing them that matters had been misrepresented,—that the Paxtoneers were a set of very worthy men (or something to that purpose) who laboured under great distress,—that Messrs. Smith &c. were come (by their own authority) as representatives, from several counties, to lay their complaints before the Legislature, and that the reason for their arming themselves was for fear of being molested or abused. By whom? Why, by the peaceable citizens of Philadelphia! Ha! ha! ha! Who can help laughing? The harangue concluded with thanks for the trouble and expense they had been at, (about nothing) and each retired to their several homes. The next day, when all was quiet, and no body dreamed of any further disturbance, we were alarmed again. The report now was, that the Paxtoneers had broke the Treaty, and were just entering the city. It is incredible to think with what alacrity the people flew to arms; in one quarter of an hour near a thousand of them were assembled, with a determination to bring the affair to a conclusion immediately, and not to suffer themselves to be harassed as they had been several days past. If the whole body of the enemy had come in, as was expected, the engagement would have been a bloody one, for the citizens were exasperated almost to madness; but happily those that appeared did not exceed thirty, (the rest having gone homewards) and as they behaved with decency they were suffered to pass without opposition. Thus the storm blew over and the inhabitants dispersed themselves.

The following day the Indians were shown to one of the men, who pretended to know the murderers, but he was unable to single them out, and declared he never remembered to have seen any of their faces before, except one old squaw; this being told to his comrades they were satisfied, and, leaving their leaders behind them to settle the other points, they marched off.

It was now hoped that all was over, but it seemed as if the very devil himself had got loose amongst us, for a boy appeared before Plumstead, and swore that himself and another boy were hired one night by some persons, with flat hats, to row four or five Indians to the Island; as soon as this was known, (which was not immediately) some people began to say, aye, there was no danger in shewing the

Indians to the Paxtoneers, after they had removed the guilty out of the way. This was a vile reflection, and bore hard both upon the Quakers and the officers who commanded at the barracks. These latter were highly incensed to think that their characters should be at the mercy of a mean boy,—and the former thought it equally cruel that the reputation of a whole society should have so slight a dependance. Application was therefore made, that the boy might be produced, and a promise was made, that he should be seen the next day at the Mayor's; but the boy disappeared, and has not been heard of since. They now say, that the Quakers have sent the boy away, to prevent a discovery of their conduct. Indeed, every thing was said that the most rancorous malice can suggest, to blacken that society. It is really amusing, to think how far our animosities are carried; persons who were intimate, now scarcely speak—or if they happen to meet and converse, presently get to quarrelling. In short, harmony and love seem to be banished from amongst us.

The Paxton Chiefs are gone home without being heard, and we are daily threatened with a return of a more formidable force. Most people are now convinced of the utility of a military force, to secure our lives and property: and the Assembly have passed a law for that purpose, which now lies before the Governor. Whether he will give his assent to it or not is doubtful, for the Assembly have vested the power of choosing officers in the people—a point which, I am confident, they will never give up so long as we remain under a Proprietory Government.

I remain thy sincere friend, &c.

[2. *Dr. John Ewing to Mr. Reed, 1764, The Frontier Point of View.* An account of the Paxton riots from the Paxton Boys's viewpoint is found in this letter written by the Reverend Dr. John Ewing, founder of the Second Presbyterian Church in Philadelphia. Joseph Reed became an influential Scotch-Irish political leader in revolutionary Pennsylvania. (William B. Reed, *Life and Correspondence of Joseph Reed*, 2 vols. [Philadelphia, 1847], I, 34-36.)

What, according to the Reverend Dr. Ewing, were the motives and aspirations of the frontiersmen?

What is said about public opinion and the Lancaster massacre?

Which of Dr. Ewing's statements conflict with statements made by other writers commenting on the riots?]

Dr. John Ewing to Mr. Reed.

Philadelphia, 1764.

As TO public affairs, our Province is greatly involved in intestine feuds, at a time, when we should rather unite, one and all, to manage the affairs of our several Governments, with prudence and discretion. A few designing men, having engrossed too much power into their

[44]

hands, are pushing matters beyond all bounds. There are twenty-two Quakers in our Assembly, at present, who, although they won't absolutely refuse to grant money for the King's use, yet never fail to contrive matters in such a manner as to afford little or no assistance to the poor distressed Frontiers; while our public money is lavishly squandered away in supporting a number of savages, who have been murdering and scalping us for many years past. This has so enraged some desperate young men, who had lost their nearest relations, by these very Indians, to cut off about twenty Indians that lived near Lancaster, who had, during the war, carried on a constant intercourse with our other enemies; and they came down to Germantown to inquire why Indians, known to be enemies, were supported, even in luxury, with the best that our markets afforded, at the public expense, while they were left in the utmost distress on the Frontiers, in want of the necessaries of life. Ample promises were made to them that their grievances should be redressed, upon which they immediately dispersed and went home. These persons have been unjustly represented as endeavouring to over- turn Government, when nothing was more distant from their minds. However this matter may be looked upon in Britain, where you know very little of the matter, you may be assured that ninety-nine in an hundred of the Province are firmly persuaded, that they are maintaining our enemies, while our friends back are suffering the greatest extremities, neglected; and that few, but Quakers, think that the Lancaster Indians have suffered any thing but their just deserts. 'Tis not a little surprising to us here, that orders should be sent from the Crown, to apprehend and bring to justice those persons who have cut off that nest of enemies that lived near Lancaster. They never were subjects to his Majesty; were a free, independent state, retaining all the powers of a free state; sat in all our Treaties with the Indians, as one of the tribes belonging to the Six Nations, in alliance with us; they entertained the French and Indian spies—gave intelligence to them of the defenceless state of our Province—furnished them with our Gazette every week, or fortnight—gave them intelligence of all the dispositions of the Province army against them—were frequently with the French and Indians at their forts and towns—supplied them with warlike stores—joined with the strange Indians in their war dances, and in the parties that made incursions on our Frontiers—were ready to take up the hatchet against the English openly, when the French requested it—actually murdered and scalped some of the Frontier inhabitants—insolently boasted of the murders they had committed, when they saw our blood was cooled, after the last Treaty at Lancaster—confessed that they had been at war with us, and would soon be at war with us again, (which accordingly happened), and even went so far as to put one of their own warriors, Jegarie, to death, because he refused to go to war with them against the English. All these things were known through the Frontier inhabitants, and are since proved upon oath. This occasioned them to be cut off by about forty or fifty persons, collected from all the Frontier counties, though they are called by the name of the little Township of Paxton, where, possibly, the smallest part of them resided.

And what surprises us more than all, the accounts we have from England, is, that our Assembly, in a petition they have drawn up, to the King, for a change of Government, should represent this Province in a state of uproar and riot, and when not a man in it has once resisted a single officer of the Government, nor a single act of violence committed, unless you call the Lancaster affair such, although it was no more than going to war with that tribe, as they had done before with others, without a formal proclamation of war by the Government. I have not time, as you may guess by this scrawl, to write more at this time, but only that I am, yours, &c.

P. S. You may publish the above account of the Lancaster Indians, if you please.

[3. *Frederick Jackson Turner, the Frontier and the Paxton Boys.* Turner set forth the main concepts behind his frontier theory in the first selection from his writings presented here. In the second, an essay on "The Old West," he discussed the colonial frontier expansion into the Old West and the significance of the Scotch-Irish pioneers, and particularly of the Paxton Boys. (Frederick Jackson Turner, "The Significance of the Frontier in American History," *Annual Report of the American Historical Association for the Year 1893* [Washington, 1894], 199-227; "The Old West," *Proceedings of the State Historical Society of Wisconsin* [Madison, 1908], pp. 184-233.)

As you read Turner, test his statements against what you have learned about the Paxton Boys.

Which of Turner's remarks are supported by the Paxton evidence? Which are contradicted or placed in doubt? Does the Paxton evidence assist you in evaluating some of Turner's statements?

What kind of judgment does the Paxton evidence permit you to make about the influence of free land on the formation of the American character?

Were the Paxton Boys more interested in killing Indians or in extending democracy? Does the evidence in this booklet support Turner's contention concerning the democratizing influence of the frontier? How do the Paxton riots represent for Turner a particular example of a wider trend in American history?]

The Significance of the Frontier in American History

FROM THE conditions of frontier life came intellectual traits of profound importance. The works of travelers along each frontier from colonial days onward describe certain common traits, and these traits have, while softening down, still persisted as survivals in the place of their origin, even when a higher social organization succeeded. The result is that to the frontier the American intellect owes its striking characteristics. That coarseness and strength combined with acuteness and inquisitiveness; that practical, inventive turn of mind, quick to find expedients; that masterful grasp of material things, lacking in the artistic but powerful to effect great ends; that restless, nervous energy; that dominant individualism, working for good and for evil, and withal that buoyancy and exuberance which comes with freedom—these are traits of the frontier, or traits called out elsewhere because of the existence of the frontier. Since the days when the fleet of Columbus sailed into the waters of the New World, America has been another name for opportunity, and the people of the United States have taken their tone from the incessant expansion which has not only been open but has even been forced upon them. He would be a rash prophet who should assert that the expansive character of American life has now entirely ceased. Movement has been its dominant fact, and, unless this training has no effect upon a people, the American energy will continually demand a wider field for its exercise. But never again will such gifts of free land offer themselves. For a moment, at the frontier, the bonds of custom are broken and unrestraint is triumphant. There is not *tabula rasa*. The stubborn American environment is there with its imperious summons to accept its conditions; the inherited ways of doing things are also there; and yet, in spite of environment, and in spite of custom, each frontier did indeed furnish a new field of opportunity, a gate of escape from the bondage of the past; and freshness, and confidence, and scorn of older society, impatience of its restraints and its ideas, and indifference to its lessons, have accompanied the frontier. What the Mediterranean Sea was to the Greeks, breaking the bond of custom, offering new experiences, calling out new institutions and activities, that, and more, the ever retreating frontier has been to the United States directly, and to the nations of Europe more remotely. And now, four centuries from the discovery of America, at the end of a hundred years of life under the Constitution, the frontier has gone, and with its going has closed the first period of American history.

The Old West

It is not the oldest West with which this chapter deals. The oldest West was the Atlantic coast. Roughly speaking, it took a century of Indian fighting and forest felling for the colonial settlements to expand into the interior to a distance of about a hundred miles from the coast. Indeed, some stretches were hardly touched in that period. This conquest of the nearest wilderness in the course of the seventeenth century and in the early years of the eighteenth, gave control of the maritime section of the nation and made way for the new movement of westward expansion. . . .

The Old West . . . in the period from about 1676 to 1763 . . . includes the back country of New England, the Mohawk Valley, the Great Valley of Pennsylvania, the Shenandoah Valley, and the Piedmont—that is, the interior or upland portion of the South lying between the Alleghanies and the head of navigation of the Atlantic rivers. . . .

Side by side with . . . German occupation of Valley and Piedmont, went the migration of the Scotch-Irish. These lowland Scots had been planted in Ulster early in the seventeenth century. Followers of John Knox, they had the contentious individualism and revolutionary temper that seem natural to Scotch Presbyterianism. They were brought up on the Old Testament, and in the doctrine of government by covenant or compact. In Ireland their fighting qualities had been revealed in the siege of Londonderry, where their stubborn resistance balked the hopes of James II. However, religious and political disabilities were imposed upon these Ulstermen, which made them discontented, and hard times contributed to detach them from their homes. Their movement to America was contemporaneous with the heavy German migration. By the Revolution, it is believed that a third of the population of Pennsylvania was Scotch-Irish. . . .

It was in Pennsylvania that the center of Scotch-Irish power lay. "These bold and indigent strangers, saying as their excuse when challenged for titles that we had solicited for colonists and they had come accordingly," and asserting that "it was against the laws of God and nature that so much land should be idle while so many christians wanted it to work on and to raise their bread," squatted on the vacant lands, especially in the region disputed between Pennsylvania and Maryland, and remained in spite of efforts to drive them off. Finding the Great Valley in the hands of the Germans, they planted their own outposts along the line of the Indian trading path from Lancaster to Bedford; they occupied Cumberland Valley, and before 1760 pressed up the Juniata somewhat beyond the narrows, spreading out along its tributaries, and by 1768 had to be warned off from the Redstone country to avoid Indian trouble. By the time of the Revolution, their settlements made Pittsburgh a center from which was to come a new era in Pennsylvania history. . . .

The creation of this frontier society—of which so large a portion differed from that of the coast in language and religion as well as in economic life, social structure, and ideals—produced an antagonism between interior and coast, which worked itself out in interesting fashion. In general this took these forms: contests between the property-holding class of the coast and the debtor class of the interior, where specie was lacking, and where paper money and a readjustment of the basis of taxation were demanded; contests over defective or unjust local government in the administration of taxes, fees, lands, and the courts; contests over apportionment in the legislature, whereby the coast was able to dominate, even when its white population was in the minority; contests to secure the complete separation of church and state; and, later, contests over slavery, internal improvements, and party politics in general. These contests are also intimately connected with the political philosophy of the Revolution and with the development of American democracy. In nearly every colony prior to the Revolution, struggles had been in progress between the party of privilege, chiefly the Eastern men of property allied with the English authorities, and the democratic classes, strongest in the West and the cities. . . .

Pennsylvania affords a clear illustration of these sectional antagonisms. The memorial of the frontier "Paxton Boys," in 1764, demanded a right to share in political privileges with the older part of the colony, and protested against the apportionment by which the counties of Chester, Bucks, and Philadelphia, together with the city of Philadelphia, elected twenty-six delegates, while the five frontier counties had but ten. The frontier complained against the failure of the dominant Quaker party of the coast to protect the interior against the Indians. The three old wealthy counties under Quaker rule feared the growth of the West, therefore made few new counties, and carefully restricted the representation in each to preserve the majority in the old section. At the same time, by a property qualification they met the danger of the democratic city population. Among the points of grievance in this colony, in addition to apportionment and representation, was the difficulty of access to the county seat, owing to the size of the back counties. Dr. Lincoln has well set forth the struggle of the back country, culminating in its triumph in the constitutional convention of 1776, which was chiefly the work of the Presbyterian counties. Indeed, there were two revolutions in Pennsylvania, which went on side by side: one a revolt against the coastal property-holding classes, the old dominant Quaker party, and the other a revolt against Great Britain, which was in this colony made possible only by the triumph of the interior.

FOR FURTHER READING

The best single account of the Paxton Riots is by Brooke Hindle, "The March of the Paxton Boys," *William and Mary Quarterly,* Third Series, III (October, 1946), 461-86. A more recent analysis of the riots, based upon further investigation, is the introduction to John R. Dunbar, ed., *The Paxton Papers* (The Hague: Martinus Nijhoff, 1957). Dunbar's volume also contains a collection of the more important pamphlets pertaining to the riots.

Dale Van Every's readable volume, *Forth to the Wilderness, The First American Frontier, 1754-1774* (New York: William Morrow and Co., 1961), shows the relationship between the riots and the westward moving frontier, and Francis Parkman's *The Conspiracy of Pontiac* (Boston: Little, Brown, 1902), II, shows how the riots were the direct result of the Indian problems emerging from the French and Indian War. Charles H. Lincoln, *The Revolutionary Movement in Pennsylvania, 1760-1776* (Philadelphia: Ginn, 1901) stresses the importance of the riots in Pennsylvania's revolutionary history. Additional brief accounts of the riots are to be found in Isaac Sharpless, *A History of the Quaker Government in Pennsylvania* (Philadelphia: T. S. Leach and Co., 1899), II, and in Wayland F. Dunaway, *The Scotch-Irish of Pennsylvania* (Chapel Hill: Univ. of North Carolina Press, 1962). Wilbur R. Jacobs, *Wilderness Politics and Indian Gifts, The Northern Colonial Frontier, 1748-1763* (Lincoln: Univ. of Nebraska Press, 1966), includes an analysis of Indian politics in the years preceding the riots, and Lawrence H. Gipson, *The British Empire Before the American Revolution, IX, The Triumphant Empire, New Responsibilities within the Enlarged Empire, 1763-1766* (New York: Knopf, 1950), emphasizes the development of an imperial Indian policy in the 1760's. Ray A. Billington, *Westward Expansion, A History of the American Frontier* (third ed.; New York: Macmillan, 1967), gives an excellent account of frontier expansion in the era before the Revolution.

Frederick Jackson Turner's seminal essay on "The Significance of the Frontier in American History," *Annual Report of the American Historical Association, 1893* (Washington: U.S. Government Printing Office, 1894), 199-227, and his essay, "The Old West," *State Historical Society of Wisconsin Proceedings* (Madison: The Society, 1908), 184-233, are reprinted in Turner, *The Frontier in American History* (New York: Holt, 1920). A recent evaluation of the frontier theory is contained in the introduction to Wilbur R. Jacobs, ed., *Frederick Jackson Turner's Legacy: Unpublished Writings in American History* (San Marino, Calif.: Huntington Library, 1965). Turner's influence upon two other leading historians of the frontier is discussed in Wilbur R. Jacobs, John W. Caughey, and Joe B. Frantz, *Turner, Bolton, and Webb: Three Historians of the Frontier* (Seattle: Univ. of Washington Press, 1965). Ray A. Billington, *The American Frontier* (second ed.; Washington: Publication No. 8, Service Center for Teachers, American Historical Association, 1965), includes an appraisal of historical literature on the frontier theory.

Three excellent volumes in the new Histories of the American Frontier series are also valuable for background reading on the Paxton Riots and the Turnerean approach to early frontier history: Ray A. Billington, *America's Frontier Heritage* (New York: Holt, Rinehart and Winston, 1966); Douglas Edward Leach, *The Northern Colonial Frontier, 1607-1763* (New York: Holt, Rinehart and Winston, 1966); and Jack M. Sosin, *The Revolutionary Frontier, 1763-1783* (New York: Holt, Rinehart and Winston, 1967).

For editorial suggestions, I am indebted to Delmer Ross, Jean Bonheim, and David Sloan.

PRINTED IN U.S.A.